1st EDITION

Perspectives on Diseases and Disorders

Huntington's Disease

Clay Farris Naff

Book Editor

Detroit • New York • San Francisco • New Haven, Conn • Waterville, Maine • London

Elizabeth Des Chenes, *Director, Publishing Solutions*

© 2012 Greenhaven Press, a part of Gale, Cengage Learning

For more information, contact:
Greenhaven Press
27500 Drake Rd.
Farmington Hills, MI 48331-3535
Or you can visit our Internet site at gale.cengage.com

For product information and technology assistance, contact us at

Gale Customer Support, 1-800-877-4253
For permission to use material from this text or product, submit all requests online at
www.cengage.com/permissions

Further permissions questions can be emailed to permissionrequest@cengage.com

Articles in Greenhaven Press anthologies are often edited for length to meet page requirements. In addition, original titles of these works are changed to clearly present the main thesis and to explicitly indicate the author's opinion. Every effort is made to ensure that Greenhaven Press accurately reflects the original intent of the authors. Every effort has been made to trace the owners of copyrighted material.

LIBRARY OF CONGRESS CATALOGING-IN-PUBLICATION DATA

Huntington's disease / Clay Farris Naff, book editor.
   p. cm. -- (Perspectives on diseases and disorders)
  Includes bibliographical references and index.
  ISBN 978-0-7377-5775-0 (hardback)
  1. Huntington's chorea--Popular works. I. Naff, Clay Farris.
  RC394.H85.H85 2012
  616.85'1--dc23
                                               2011052230

Printed in the United States of America
1 2 3 4 5 6 7 16 15 14 13 12

CONTENTS

Laboratory have succeeded in capturing an image of the misshapen protein named huntingtin.

National Institute of Neurological Disorders and Stroke

Until recently Huntington's disease remained largely mysterious, but medical research has been making progress toward treatment and a possible cure.

CHAPTER 2   Controversies Concerning
                Huntington's Disease

Eryn Brown

Despite reluctance, there are good reasons for people to be aware if they have the gene that leads to Huntington's disease.

Laura Spinney

Various reasons, including a wish not to know that oneself or a loved one has a fatal, incurable disease and the desire to conceal such information from health insurance companies, contribute to the possibility that the incidence of Huntington's disease is higher than reported.

Quinn Eastman

By genetically engineering monkeys to develop Huntington's disease, scientists may have a unique way to test potential treatments.

Charlotte Raven

A woman who was diagnosed with Huntington's disease shortly after giving birth to her daughter contemplates suicide in the face of the disease.

FOREWORD

"Medicine, to produce health, has to examine disease."
—Plutarch

Independent research on a health issue is often the first step to complement discussions with a physician. But locating accurate, well-organized, understandable medical information can be a challenge. A simple Internet search on terms such as "cancer" or "diabetes," for example, returns an intimidating number of results. Sifting through the results can be daunting, particularly when some of the information is inconsistent or even contradictory. The Greenhaven Press series Perspectives on Diseases and Disorders offers a solution to the often overwhelming nature of researching diseases and disorders.

From the clinical to the personal, titles in the Perspectives on Diseases and Disorders series provide students and other researchers with authoritative, accessible information in unique anthologies that include basic information about the disease or disorder, controversial aspects of diagnosis and treatment, and first-person accounts of those impacted by the disease. The result is a well-rounded combination of primary and secondary sources that, together, provide the reader with a better understanding of the disease or disorder.

Each volume in Perspectives on Diseases and Disorders explores a particular disease or disorder in detail. Material for each volume is carefully selected from a wide range of sources, including encyclopedias, journals, newspapers, nonfiction books, speeches, government documents, pamphlets, organization newsletters, and position papers. Articles in the first chapter provide an authoritative, up-to-date overview that covers symptoms, causes and effects, treatments, cures, and medical advances. The second chapter presents a substantial number of opposing viewpoints on controversial treatments and other current debates relating to the volume topic. The third chapter offers a variety of personal perspectives on the disease or disorder. Patients, doctors, caregivers, and loved ones represent just some of the voices found in this narrative chapter.

Each Perspectives on Diseases and Disorders volume also includes:

- An **annotated table of contents** that provides a brief summary of each article in the volume.
- An **introduction** specific to the volume topic.
- Full-color **charts and graphs** to illustrate key points, concepts, and theories.
- Full-color **photos** that show aspects of the disease or disorder and enhance textual material.
- **"Fast Facts"** that highlight pertinent additional statistics and surprising points.
- A **glossary** providing users with definitions of important terms.
- A **chronology** of important dates relating to the disease or disorder.
- An annotated list of **organizations to contact** for students and other readers seeking additional information.
- A **bibliography** of additional books and periodicals for further research.
- A detailed **subject index** that allows readers to quickly find the information they need.

Whether a student researching a disorder, a patient recently diagnosed with a disease, or an individual who simply wants to learn more about a particular disease or disorder, a reader who turns to Perspectives on Diseases and Disorders will find a wealth of information in each volume that offers not only basic information, but also vigorous debate from multiple perspectives.

INTRODUCTION

What do you do when there's practically no hope? That's a question Huntington's disease (HD) forces victims and their loved ones to confront. The inherited brain disease is so implacable, its course so degrading and deadly, and its treatments so scanty and feeble that most people at risk avoid being tested. They do not want to know.

For those who learn—either by diagnostic test or by the onset of symptoms that cannot be ignored—that they have HD, the question looms. Perhaps the only good that comes of this terrible disease lies in the magnificent human spirit it rouses in so many.

Six-year-old Landon Hansen of Sioux Falls, South Dakota, is not ready to give up. When his big sister was diagnosed with early onset HD, he created a fund-raising campaign to, in his words, "kick Juvenile Huntington's butt!"[1] He is giving out buttons in return for contributions for research to find a cure for the fatal condition.

Huntington's disease lurks in the genes. Unlike recessive disorders, a child can inherit HD from just one afflicted parent and has a fifty-fifty chance of doing so. It typically begins to manifest itself in twitches and jerks. These involuntary movements led to the original name of the malady: Huntington's chorea (meaning "dance"). The spasms are followed by increasing difficulty in walking. Cognitive dysfunction follows: Memory lapses, speech impairment, personality changes, violent rage, and depression are common symptoms. The victim suffers a growing inability to think straight, communicate clearly, or make plans, even as the body becomes more and more spastic and useless. Unless suicide or fatal accident intervenes first, premature death after a long and debilitating decline invariably follows.

Most often those who are fated to come down with HD begin to exhibit its signs in their middle years, starting at about age thirty-five. There are rarely any symptoms during childhood, but the disease can emerge as early as age two. When it takes a grip in youth, the victim rarely survives to adulthood.

The disease was first characterized by George Huntington in 1872, when modern medicine was in its infancy and genetics hardly known. As recounted by physician and lawyer John P. Conomy, Huntington was an unlikely discoverer. Just a year out of medical school,

> [the] young family practitioner of the small Ohio River city of Pomeroy, Ohio, traveled over the bleak countryside five miles to the larger town of Middleport, Ohio to address the local medical society. . . . His brief, uniformly anecdotal and entirely unreferenced address, not suffering publication delay, was put eight weeks later in the *Medical and Surgical Reporter* of Philadelphia. This has become one of the classical descriptions of neurological disease. George Huntington dealt with hereditary chorea as a reminiscence of his childhood spent on the eastern extremity of Long Island (New York), where, as the son and grandson of physicians, he recalled patients from his father's practice.[2]

Following that initial identification of the disease, researchers worked hard to uncover its cause. However, it took well over a century to tease it out. In 1993 scientists at last succeeded in isolating the gene on chromosome 4 that causes all the trouble. The gene, now known as huntingtin, encodes directions for the production of a protein of the same name, whose exact function is still unknown. What researchers found, however, was that in HD patients and carriers, the gene has a characteristic error: excess repetitions of a triplet of DNA bases spelling out CAG.

In a normal huntingtin gene, this CAG sequence repeats eleven to twenty-nine times. In the mutant gene the repetition is extended up to eighty times, with terrible consequences. It causes the huntingtin protein to fold into the wrong shape, leading to clumps of protein in the brain and the death of nearby brain cells.

Despite this fairly detailed discovery of HD pathology, virtually no progress has been made in treating the disease. At best, physicians are able to ease a few of the symptoms with medications that relieve depression or calm the twitching.

Is it any wonder that the suicide rate skyrockets among HD patients? Estimates vary, but at least one study finds a more than eightfold increase in suicides among those who suspect or learn that they have HD. That amounts to an estimated 2 to 3 percent of HD patients who take their own lives.

Perhaps the real wonder is that it is not higher still. In a study of more than four thousand HD patients, Jane S. Paulsen and her fellow researchers found that nearly a quarter consider suicide when they feel themselves to be at risk of the disease and that about 22 percent contemplate ending their lives as the debilitating symptoms set in.

In a publication of the Huntington's Disease Society of America, a middle-aged woman known only as Lisa speaks bluntly about the choice: "Why would I want to continue living without a brain receptive to the beauties of life, to the feelings and to the needs of others? Why would I want to spend the rest of my days, or years, just eating and sleeping, and waiting? Waiting for the end to come finally? What is the point?"[3]

Another at-risk man, anonymously seeking advice on the Internet, recalled how his mother reacted to her diagnosis: "I came home from college one summer to my mom who had just taken a test for Huntington's. Her father and brother suffered and died from it, so she wanted to get tested. She tested positive. Shortly thereafter she exhibited signs of the disease, suffered severe anxiety, and committed suicide. My sister and I have not been tested, and live with a fifty percent chance of manifesting the disease."[4]

In the face of such grim, seemingly unshakable fates, it is inspiring to find that so many persevere and make the best they can of it. Jerry Dean Nichols Jr. of Marshalltown, Iowa, always knew his chances of living a long and normal life were no better than fifty-fifty. The father after whom he was named began his struggle with HD when Jerry was just two. He grew up seeing his own dismal fate enacted day by day before his eyes. Yet rather than give in to despair, Jerry became a helper to others under the most difficult circumstances: He joined the army as a medic. After three years, his service was cut short by the onset of debilitating symptoms, and thereafter he struggled with the disease for sixteen years until his death at age forty. Family members said he remained cheerful throughout, relying on faith, family, and friends to endure the unendurable.

His is not the only story of remarkable courage in the face of implacable doom. Rebecca Potter, a British schoolteacher, took one of the most life-affirming steps possible in response to learning that she has HD: She got married. Potter says:

> My philosophy on life was and still is to live it to the full and to enjoy each single day. I know that HD will probably kill me, but I am not dead yet and will fight the disease every step of the way. Since being diagnosed I have had to retire from teaching, but a few months after my test result I met and subsequently married my husband. I told him early in our relationship about my diagnosis and he married me aware of the future; I accept that not all men would do this but there is hope! We have been married for nearly two years and our first baby is due in March.[5]

In short, Potter declares, life goes on.

Although a cure for HD remains out of reach, medical science has made progress. Treatment with fetal stem cells has shown promising results. Injected into the brain in areas devastated by HD, the stem cells blossom into new brain cells that take the place of those killed off by the disease. Recent research in mice suggests that supplements of melatonin, a naturally occurring hormone, can delay and dampen the symptoms of HD. Other labs are exploring the possibility of using new gene-silencing techniques to turn off the harmful CAG repeats in the genes of HD patients. These and other lines of research may eventually converge on a cure. Those who are in the early stages now can only hope that such a deeply needed development will come in time.

An illustration shows diseased bone marrow being treated using a fetal stem cell transplant. In the case of Huntington's disease, fetal stem cells are grafted directly onto the areas of the brain affected by the disease.
(© BSIP/Photo Researchers, Inc.)

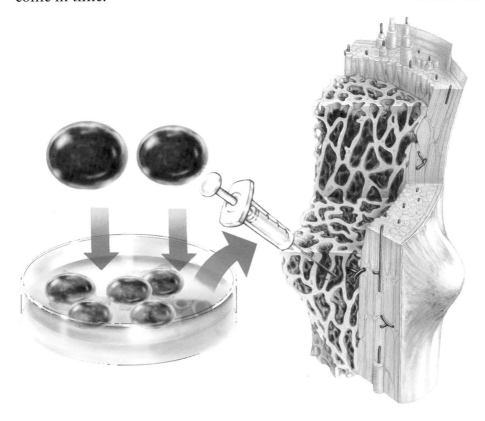

Notes

1. Quoted in Jennifer Hudspeth, "Button Boy Crusades to Help Save His Sister," KDLT News, October 19, 2011. www.kdlt.com/index.php?option=com_content&task=view&id=12750&Itemid=57.

2. John P. Conomy, "Dr. George Huntington and the Disease Bearing His Name," Huntington's Disease Society of America, Northeast Ohio Chapter. www.lkwdpl.org/hdsa/conomy.htm.

3. Quoted in Allen J. Rubin, "Suicide and Huntington's Disease," *Horizon*, 1993.

4. Gorilla55, "I Am a Man Whose Mom Tested Positive," Reddit, October 9, 2011. www.reddit.com/r/lAmA/comments/I5oz6/iama_man_whose_mom_tested_positive_for.

5. Rebecca Potter, "I Have Huntington's Disease, but I Can Still Live Life to the Full," *Guardian* (Manchester, UK), January 27, 2010. www.guardian.co.uk/commentisfree/2010/jan/28/response-huntingtons-disease-cure.

CHAPTER 1

Understanding Huntington's Disease

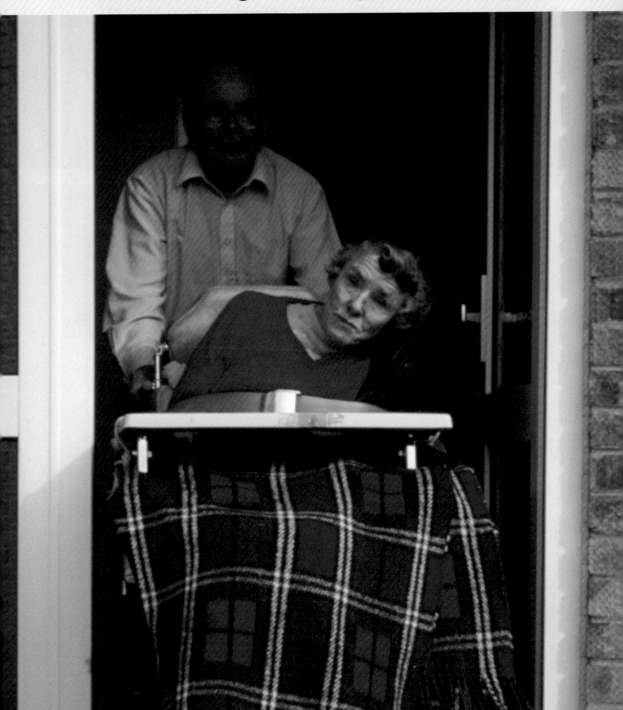

An Overview of Huntington's Disease

Laith Farid Gulli and Rebecca J. Frey

Huntington's (or Huntington) disease is a deadly neurological disorder. In the following selection Laith Farid Gulli and Rebecca J. Frey present a comprehensive overview of the disease. The name, they explain, has evolved from an earlier version that included the Greek word for *dance*, a reflection of the involuntary movements that overtake a victim of Huntington's disease. But there is more to Huntington's disease than loss of motor control. It also ravages the brain, leading to changes in personality and cognitive function. The cause of this terrible affliction, they explain, is a defective gene, which in turn leads to the production of a malformed protein that is the immediate source of the damage. A genetic test can identify the disease, but there is virtually nothing that can stop its progression. Huntington's disease has no cure, and only minor treatments such as exercise and physical therapy exist. These can help a patient cope with symptoms, but they cannot prevent the slow decline into death that invariably accompanies the disease. Gulli is a physician who practices as a psychotherapist in Michigan. Frey is a medical writer.

SOURCE: Laith Farid Gulli and Rebecca J. Frey, "Huntington Disease," *The Gale Encyclopedia of Medicine,* 4E. Copyright © 2011 Gale, a part of Cengage Learning, Inc. Reproduced by permission. www.cengage.com/permissions.

Photo on previous page. Caused by a defective gene, Huntington's disease is a progressive neurodegenerative disease causing uncontrolled physical movements and mental deterioration. (© Conor Caffrey/Photo Researchers, Inc.)

Huntington disease (HD) is a progressive neurode-generative disease causing uncontrolled physical movements and mental deterioration. The disease was discovered by George Sumner Huntington (1850–1916), an Ohio doctor who first described the hereditary movement disorder in 1872.

Huntington disease is also called Huntington chorea or hereditary chorea. The word chorea comes from the Greek word for "dance" and refers to the involuntary movements of the patient's feet, lower arms, and face that develop as the disease progresses. It is occasionally referred to as "Woody Guthrie's disease" for the American folksinger who died from it. Huntington disease (HD) causes progressive loss of cells in areas of the brain responsible for certain aspects of movement control and mental abilities. A person with HD gradually develops abnormal movements and changes in cognition (thinking), behavior and personality.

Huntington's disease is occasionally referred to as "Woody Guthrie's disease" for the legendary American folksinger who died from it. (© Michael Ochs Archives/Getty Images)

The onset of symptoms of HD usually occurs between the ages of 30 and 50; although in 10% of cases, onset is in late childhood or early adolescence. Approximately 30,000 people in the United States are affected by HD, with another 150,000 at risk for developing this disorder. The frequency of HD is 4–7 cases per 100,000 persons.

A Defective Gene Is to Blame

Huntington disease is caused by a defect in the HD gene (an inherited unit which contains a code for a protein), which is located on the short arm of chromosome 4. The gene codes for a protein called huntingtin, whose function is not known as of early 2005. The nucleotide codes (building blocks of genes arranged in a specific code which chemically forms into proteins), contain CAG repeats (40 or more of these repeat sequences). The extra building blocks in the huntingtin gene cause the protein that is made from it to contain an extra section as well. It is currently thought that this extra protein section, or portion, interacts with other proteins in brain cells where it occurs, and that this interaction ultimately leads to cell death.

The HD gene is a dominant gene, meaning that only one copy of it is needed to develop the disease. HD affects both males and females. The gene may be inherited from either parent, who will also be affected by the disease. A parent with the HD gene has a 50% chance of passing it on to each offspring. The chances of passing on the HD gene are not affected by the results of previous pregnancies.

The symptoms of HD fall into three categories: motor or movement symptoms; personality and behavioral changes; and cognitive decline. The severity and rate of progression of each type of symptom can vary from person to person.

Early motor symptoms include restlessness, twitching and a desire to move about. Handwriting may become less controlled, and coordination may decline. Later symptoms include:

- dystonia, or sustained abnormal postures, including facial grimaces, a twisted neck, or an arched back
- chorea, in which involuntary jerking, twisting or writhing motions become pronounced
- slowness of voluntary movements, inability to regulate the speed or force of movements, inability to initiate movement and slowed reactions
- difficulty speaking and swallowing due to involvement of the throat muscles
- localized or generalized weakness and impaired balance ability
- rigidity, especially in late-stage disease

Personality and behavioral changes include depression, irritability, anxiety and apathy. The person with HD may become impulsive, aggressive, or socially withdrawn.

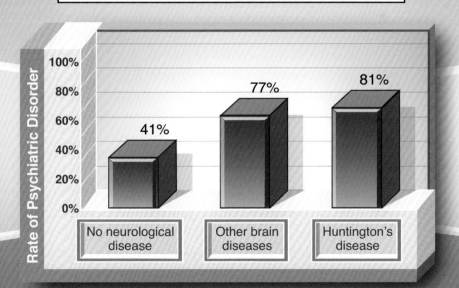

Huntington's Disease Patients Have More Psychiatric Disorders

Rate of Psychiatric Disorder

- No neurological disease — 41%
- Other brain diseases — 77%
- Huntington's disease — 81%

Taken from: I. Leroi et al. "Psychopathology in Patients with Degenerative Cerebellar Diseases: A Comparison to Huntington's Disease," *American Journal of Psychiatry*, August 2002.

Cognitive changes include loss of ability to plan and execute routine tasks, slowed thought, and impaired or inappropriate judgment. Short-term memory loss usually occurs, although long-term memory is usually not affected. The person with late-stage HD usually retains knowledge of his environment and recognizes family members or other loved ones, despite severe cognitive decline.

Diagnosing the Disease

Diagnosis of HD begins with a detailed medical history, and a thorough physical and neurological examination. The family's medical history is very important. Magnetic resonance imaging (MRI) or computed tomography scan (CT scan) imaging may be performed to look for degeneration in the basal ganglia and cortex, the brain regions most affected in HD.

Physicians have recently developed a Uniform Huntington's Disease Rating Scale, or UHDRS, to assess a patient's symptoms and the speed of progression of the disease.

A genetic test is available for confirmation of the clinical diagnosis. In this test, a small blood sample is taken, and DNA from it is analyzed to determine the CAG repeat number. A person with a repeat number of 30 or below will not develop HD. A person with a repeat number between 35 and 40 may not develop the disease within their normal lifespan. A person with a very high number of repeats (70 or above) is likely to develop the juvenile-onset form. An important part of genetic testing is extensive genetic counseling.

Prenatal testing is available. A person at risk for HD (a child of an affected person) may obtain fetal testing without determining whether she herself carries the gene. This test, also called a linkage test, examines the pattern of DNA near the gene in both parent and fetus, but does not analyze for the triple nucleotide repeat (CAG). If the DNA patterns do not match, the fetus can be assumed not to have inherited the HD gene, even if present in the parent. A pattern match indicates the fetus probably has the same genetic makeup of the at-risk parent.

There Is No Cure Available

There is no cure for HD, nor any treatment that can slow the rate of progression. Treatment is aimed at reducing the disability caused by the motor impairments, and treating behavioral and emotional symptoms.

Physical therapy is used to maintain strength and compensate for lost strength and balance. Stretching and range of motion exercises help minimize contracture, or muscle shortening, a result of weakness and disuse. The physical therapist also advises on the use of mobility aids such as walkers or wheelchairs.

Motor symptoms may be treated with drugs, although some studies suggest that anti-chorea treatment rarely improves function. Chorea (movements caused by abnormal muscle contractions) can be suppressed with drugs that deplete dopamine, an important brain chemical regulating movement. As HD progresses, natural dopamine levels fall, leading to loss of chorea and an increase in rigidity and movement slowness. Treatment with L-dopa (which resupplies dopamine) may be of some value. Frequent reassessment of the effectiveness and appropriateness of any drug therapy is necessary.

Occupational therapy is used to design compensatory strategies for lost abilities in the activities of daily living, such as eating, dressing, and grooming. The occupational therapist advises on modifications to the home that improve safety, accessibility, and comfort.

Difficulty swallowing may be lessened by preparation of softer foods, blending food in an electric blender, and taking care to eat slowly and carefully. Use of a straw for

> **FAST FACT**
>
> An estimated two hundred thousand Americans are at risk of inheriting Huntington's disease from an affected parent.

all liquids can help. The potential for choking on food is a concern, especially late in the disease progression. Caregivers should learn the use of the Heimlich maneuver. In addition, passage of food into the airways increases the risk for pneumonia. A gastric feeding tube may be needed, if swallowing becomes too difficult or dangerous.

Speech difficulties may be partially compensated by using picture boards or other augmentative communication devices. Loss of cognitive ability affects both speech production and understanding. A speech-language pathologist can work with the family to develop simplified and more directed communication strategies, including speaking slowly, using simple words, and repeating sentences exactly.

Early behavioral changes, including depression and anxiety, may respond to drug therapy. Maintaining a calm, familiar, and secure environment is useful as the disease progresses. Support groups for both patients and caregivers form an important part of treatment. . . .

Psychotherapy is often recommended for individuals who know themselves to be at risk for the disease. Some persons want to know their risk status while others prefer not to be tested. Psychotherapy may be useful in helping at-risk persons decide about testing as well as coping with the results of the test.

A Slow Decline

The person with Huntington disease may be able to maintain a job for several years after diagnosis, despite the increase in disability. Loss of cognitive functions and increase in motor and behavioral symptoms eventually prevent the person with HD from continuing employment. Ultimately, severe motor symptoms prevent mobility. Death usually occurs between 10 and 30 years after disease onset, typically as the result of pneumonia or a fall. Progressive weakness of respiratory and swallowing muscles leads to increased risk of respiratory infection and choking, the most common causes of death.

Venezuela Village Holds Cure for Hereditary Illness

Benedict Mander

It has long been known that Huntington's disease is an inherited neurological disease, but no one knew precisely what the cause might be. In the following selection journalist Benedict Mander reports on the woman who ended the mystery. Nancy Wexler, whose own mother developed Huntington's disease, began studying the people of a village in Venezuela where the incidence of the disease is extraordinarily high. By taking blood samples from some of the people in the village, she was able to launch a search for the cause. Along with other scientists in the United States, Wexler and her colleagues ultimately identified the single abnormal gene that leads to Huntington's disease. They isolated the Huntington's disease gene on chromosome 4. It codes for production of a protein called huntingtin, the normal function of which is still unknown but which in the defective version produces the debilitating disease.

  Mander is the Venezuela and Caribbean correspondent for the *Financial Times*. He has been based in Caracas since 2007.

It does not take long to realise that there is something wrong in Barranquitas. Some of the villagers wander around aimlessly, looking confused and frightened. Many are grotesquely emaciated. Their limbs jerk erratically.

A grim fate awaits many of the inhabitants of this isolated village on the south western shores of Lake Maracaibo in Venezuela, even those who appear perfectly healthy.

About half of the roughly 10,000-strong population of Barranquitas either has, or is at risk of developing, Huntington's disease (HD), a fatal hereditary illness that gradually kills brain cells and causes the body to waste away.

This remote area has the highest concentration of HD in the world, which is why Professor Nancy Wexler has come here almost every year since 1979. It was her research, far away from the cutting-edge laboratories of the developed world, that was the key to a discovery that pushed back the boundaries of science.

"It was this family here that launched the Human Genome Project," says Prof Wexler, her arm affectionately around the shoulder of a young man called Siros. "Siros's family proved that we had the gene," she explains, from a dingy concrete room in Siros's home in Barranquitas.

By studying the blood samples from Siros's family, which has been afflicted with a uniquely large number of cases of HD through several generations (both of Siros's parents suffered from the disease, as did 10 of their 14 children), Prof Wexler and her collaborators isolated the gene that carries the disease.

"They said it would be like trying to find a needle in a haystack. Actually, it's more like trying to find a particular bit of hay in a haystack," says Prof Wexler. She said that most scientists ridiculed her quest, while even the "believers" warned that the project could take anything from 50 to 100 years.

But she was determined: when Prof Wexler was in her early 20s her mother was diagnosed with HD, meaning

Estimated Incidence of Huntington's Disease: A Comparison

Cases of Huntington's Disease in Barranquitas, Venezuela, versus the United States:

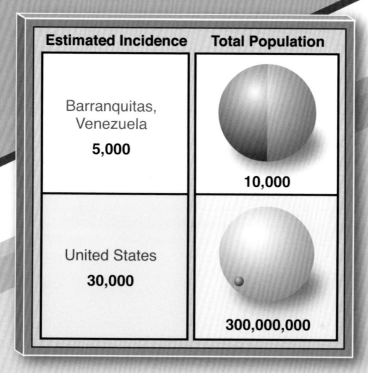

Estimated Incidence	Total Population
Barranquitas, Venezuela **5,000**	10,000
United States **30,000**	300,000,000

Taken from: eMedTV, based on data from Benedict Mander, *Financial Times* (London), August 17, 2010. www.emedtv.com and www.ft.com.

that she herself has a one-in-two chance of developing the disease.

Prof Wexler's research, which included painstakingly piecing together family relations in Barranquitas and a nearby village called Laguneta, enabled the discovery of the gene that causes HD.

Her ground-breaking methods proved that it was possible to do the same with all genes, heralding the beginning of the Human Genome Project. "It was mind-blowing," she said. The discovery of the HD gene also meant that accurate tests could be made to determine whether or not humans, including foetuses, would develop the disease.

Prof Wexler decided not to take the test herself. "What's the point of finding out whether I have the disease if there's no cure?" she asks.

So far a cure has remained elusive. Not only would it change the lives of a huge number of people around the world—HD occurs in 5–10 people per 100,000—but it is also believed that a cure for HD might help in finding a cure for other more complex neurodegenerative disorders such as Parkinson's and Alzheimer's.

So Prof Wexler keeps returning to Barranquitas, where she has become known as the "blonde angel". Now, wherever

A technician for the Human Genome Project demonstrates the matrix-assisted laser desorption ionization machine. Researchers use the device to analyze a patient's DNA code to determine the risk for Huntington's and other diseases. (**© Larry Downing/Reuters/ Landov**)

she goes in this rundown, forgotten place, she is greeted with smiles, hugs and cheers, and attracts large crowds that follow her around its muddy streets.

"She's like the Pied Piper," remarked the former British Ambassador to Venezuela, Catherine Royle, who has closely supported Prof Wexler's work.

Although companies such as Shell and Glaxo-Smith-Kline have shown support, if so far limited, for the project, perhaps the biggest barrier to progress is posed by the Venezuelan government. Permission is required to take blood samples out of the country to continue research, which is essential since no laboratory in Venezuela has the technology to do so.

FAST FACT

The gene that causes Huntington's disease was discovered in 1993.

The government's response has been lukewarm. There are further concerns that if the government does decide to take over the project, it will soon be forgotten and go the way of so many other poorly managed government-run ventures.

That is a prospect that dismays those who work in the field, such as María Luisa Hernández, a local who cares for children in danger of developing HD.

"Nancy Wexler has given more than just professional help but her love, her life. We also have a strong sense of community here. But we need more than that: we need support [from the state]."

The Diagnosis of Huntington's Disease May Become Easier

Cell Press

While many mysteries remain unsolved concerning Huntington's disease, one thing is clear: The neurological condition's most immediate cause is a malformed protein called huntingtin. The function of the healthy version of the protein remains largely unknown, but the malformed version causes the terrible and ultimately fatal symptoms associated with Huntington's disease. The following article from Cell Press, featured on the ScienceDaily website, describes how scientists are uncovering other functions of the huntingtin protein. Swedish researcher Åsa Petersén and her team have discovered that it leads to changes in appetite. The symptom results from changes in the hypothalamus triggered by huntingtin. Scientists hope that this research may provide another avenue for early diagnosis. Cell Press develops and publishes scientific journals. ScienceDaily is an award-winning science news website.

SOURCE: Cell Press, "Huntington's Disease Protein Has Broader Effects on Brain, Study Shows," ScienceDaily, April 5, 2011. Originally printed as Sofia Hult, Rana Soylu, Tomas Björklund, Bengt F. Belgardt, Jan Mauer, Jens C. Brüning, Deniz Kirik, Åsa Petersén, "Mutant Huntingtin Causes Metabolic Imbalance by Disruption of Hypothalamic Neurocircuits," *Cell Metabolism*, 2011; 13 (4): 428–39 DOI: 10.1016/j.cmet.2011.02.013. Copyright © 2011 by Elsevier.

In Huntington's disease, the mutant protein known as huntingtin leads to the degeneration of a part of the brain known as the basal ganglia, causing the motor disturbances that represent one of the most defining features of the fatal disease. But a new study reported in the April issue of *Cell Metabolism*, a Cell Press publication, shows that the mutant protein also is responsible for metabolic imbalances in the hypothalamus, a brain region that plays an important role in appetite control.

"This helps to explain metabolic changes and increases in appetite that have been observed in people at the early stages of disease," even before any motor symptoms appear, said Åsa Petersén of Lund University in Sweden. "It should encourage us to do more clinical studies. If we really understand the pathways that are affected, it may lead to new targets for intervention."

Broad Range of Symptoms

The clinical diagnosis of Huntington's disease is based entirely on the presence of overt motor dysfunction. But, in fact, Petersén said, the original publication that defined the disease back in 1872 described a wide spectrum of problems: motor abnormalities, depression, cognitive decline and changes in body weight among them. Subsequent studies of the Huntington's brain traced the motor disturbances to massive losses of the basal ganglia. "Those findings overshadowed other changes," Petersén said.

> ## FAST FACT
>
> The mutant protein huntingtin leads to the loss of up to 25 percent of brain cells.

But Petersén spends half of her time working as a clinician. She sees people with a diagnosis of Huntington's disease and carriers of the disease—people who know they carry the mutant gene and are therefore guaranteed to get the disease but who don't yet have any motor symptoms at all. "They complain about other symptoms," she said, including depression, anxiety, sleep disturbances and increases in appetite and weight.

This illustration shows the structures that make up the basal ganglia, which are responsible for motor disturbances (involuntary bodily movements). The basal ganglia are abnormal in individuals with Huntington's disease. (© Peter Gardiner/Photo Researchers, Inc.)

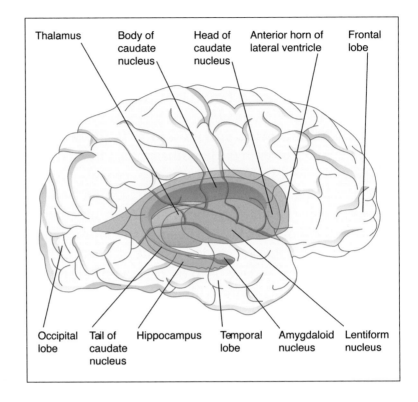

Thalamus Body of caudate nucleus Head of caudate nucleus Anterior horn of lateral ventricle Frontal lobe

Occipital lobe Tail of caudate nucleus Hippocampus Temporal lobe Amygdaloid nucleus Lentiform nucleus

Those anecdotes led her to suspect that the mutant protein, which is ubiquitously expressed, might have effects on other parts of the brain, and the hypothalamus in particular. In an earlier study, she examined the brains of Huntington's carriers to find structural changes in the hypothalamus that could be observed 10 years before motor symptoms set in, along with shifts in brain chemistry.

Work Began with Mice

In the new study, Petersén and her colleagues set out to confirm that those metabolic abnormalities are due to the effects of mutant huntingtin. First they showed that mice with Huntington's disease develop impaired glucose metabolism along with pronounced resistance to insulin and the fat hormone leptin. Those metabolic symptoms could be reproduced in mice that only expressed the mutant huntingtin in the hypothalamus. When the researchers disabled the mutant huntingtin protein only in the hypothalamus, those metabolic disturbances disappeared.

"Our findings establish a causal link between mutant huntingtin expression in the hypothalamus and metabolic dysfunction," the researchers wrote. They also suggest that metabolic parameters could serve as powerful readouts for assessing therapies aimed at treating the disease by targeting the mutant protein in the brain.

Petersén says she suspects the mutant huntingtin will ultimately be found to influence other processes, both in the brain and in other tissues. She has plans to further explore

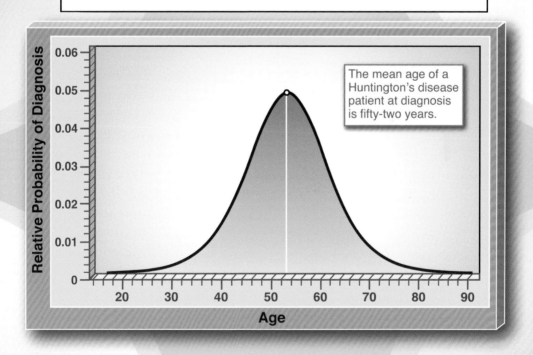

Huntington's Disease: Age at Diagnosis

The mean age of a Huntington's disease patient at diagnosis is fifty-two years.

Relative Probability of Diagnosis / Age

the connection between the mutant protein and the depression, anxiety and other symptoms that also may be early signs of the disease.

In the broader scheme of things, she says the new findings highlight the important links between the study of metabolism and neuroscience. "There's a lot to be gained through cross-fertilization between the two fields," she said.

Scientists Image the Protein Responsible for Huntington's Disease Symptoms

Agatha Bardoel

The most immediate cause of Huntington's disease is a malformed protein known as huntingtin. Learning about the protein has been extremely challenging, because it is so tiny and complex. In the following selection, however, Agatha Bardoel reports on a breakthrough at the Oak Ridge National Laboratory. Researchers there have used a neutron-scattering device to image the protein in the early stages of disease formation. Neutrons are subatomic particles that carry no charge. Using the Bio-SANS instrument, researchers were able to get a series of snapshots of the protein taking shape. By studying images of how the rogue protein forms, researchers hope they can develop drugs with highly specific actions designed to counteract the disease-causing pathways. Oak Ridge National Laboratory is a Tennessee-based federal science project of the Department of Energy that applies nuclear technologies to advance research. Bardoel is a science writer employed in public information at Oak Ridge National Laboratory.

SOURCE: Agatha Bardoel, "Neutrons Provide First Sub-nanoscale Snapshots of Huntington's Disease Protein," Oak Ridge National Laboratory, May 19, 2011.

Researchers at the Department of Energy's Oak Ridge National Laboratory [ORNL] and the University of Tennessee [UT] Medical Center have for the first time successfully characterized the earliest structural formation of the disease type of the protein that causes Huntington's disease. The incurable, hereditary neurological disorder is always fatal and affects one in 10,000 Americans.

Huntington's disease is caused by a renegade protein "huntingtin" that destroys neurons in areas of the brain concerned with the emotions, intellect and movement. All humans have the normal huntingtin protein, which is known to be essential to human life, although its true biological functions remain unclear.

Using Neutrons to Capture Images

Christopher Stanley, a Shull Fellow in the Neutron Scattering Science Division at ORNL, and Valerie Berthelier, a UT Graduate School of Medicine researcher who studies

Researchers at the Oak Ridge National Laboratory have used a neutron-scattering device on patients in the early stages of Huntington's disease to image the protein that causes the illness. (© AP Images/ Knoxville News Sentinel, Michael Patrick)

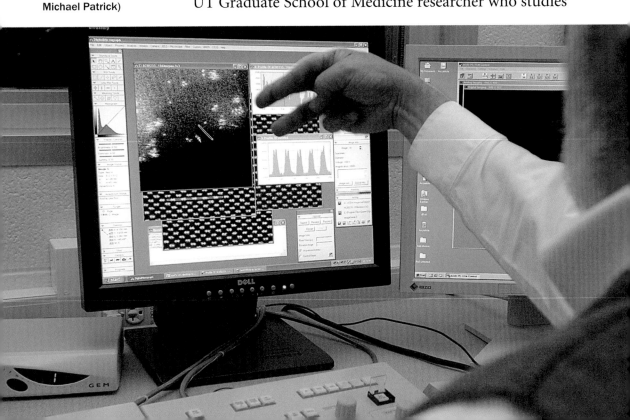

protein folding and misfolding in Huntington's, have used a small-angle neutron scattering instrument, called Bio-SANS, at ORNL's High Flux Isotope Reactor [HFIR] to explore the earliest aggregate species of the protein that are believed to be the most toxic.

Stanley and Berthelier, in research published today [May 18, 2011] in *Biophysical Journal*, were able to determine the size and mass of the mutant protein structures—from the earliest small, spherical precursor species composed of two and three peptides [compounds of two or more amino acids]—along the aggregation pathway to the development of the resulting, later-stage fibrils [threadlike structures]. They were also able to see inside the later-stage fibrils and determine their internal structure, which provides additional insight into how the peptides aggregate.

> **FAST FACT**
>
> People who have forty or more repeats of the amino acid glutamine in their huntingtin protein are virtually certain to develop Huntington's disease if they live a normal life span.

"Bio-SANS is a great instrument for taking time-resolved snapshots. You can look at how this stuff changes as a function of time and be able to catch the structures at the earliest of times," Stanley said. "When you study several of these types of systems with different glutamines or different conditions, you begin to learn more and more about the nature of these aggregates and how they begin forming."

Too Many Glutamines

Normal huntingtin contains a region of 10 to 20 glutamine amino acids in succession. However, the DNA of Huntington's disease patients encodes for 37 or more glutamines, causing instability in huntingtin fragments that contain this abnormally long glutamine repeat. Consequentially, the mutant protein fragment cannot be degraded normally and instead forms deposits of fibrils in neurons.

Those deposits, or clumps, were originally seen as the cause of the devastation that ensues in the brain. More recently researchers think the clumping may actually be a kind of biological housecleaning, an attempt by the brain cells to clean out these toxic proteins from places where they are destructive. Stanley and Berthelier set out to learn through neutron scattering what the toxic proteins were and when and where they occurred.

The Scale of Things

Size of the Nanoscale

Just how small is "nano"? In the International System of Units, the prefix "nano" means one-billionth; therefore, one nanometer is one-billionth of a meter. It is difficult to imagine just how small that is, so here are some examples.

- A sheet of paper is about 100,000 nanometers thick.

- A strand of human DNA is 2.5 nanometers in diameter.

- There are 25,400,000 nanometers in one inch.

- A human hair is approximately 80,000 nanometers wide.

- A single gold atom is about a third of a nanometer in diameter.

- On a comparative scale if the diameter of a marble was one nanometer, the diameter of the earth would be about one meter.

- One nanometer is about as long as your fingernail grows in one second.

Taken from: National Nanotechnology Initiative, "Size of the Nanoscale," www.nano.gov.

At the HFIR Bio-SANS instrument, the neutron beam comes through a series of mirrors that focus it on the sample. The neutrons interact with the sample, providing data on its atomic structure, and then the neutrons scatter, to be picked up by a detector. From the data the detector sends of the scattering pattern, researchers can deduce at a scale of less than billionths of a meter the size and shape of the diseased, aggregating protein, at each time-step along its growth pathway.

SANS was able to distinguish the small peptide aggregates in the sample solution from the rapidly forming and growing larger aggregates that are simultaneously present. In separate experiments, they were able to monitor the disappearance of the single peptides, as well as the formation of the mature fibrils.

Potential to Detoxify Huntingtin

Now that they know the structures, the hope is to develop drugs that can counteract the toxic properties in the early stages, or dissuade them from taking the path to toxicity. "The next step would be, let's take drug molecules and see how they can interact and affect these structures," Stanley said.

For now, the researchers believe Bio-SANS will be useful in the further study of Huntington's disease aggregates and applicable for the study of other protein aggregation processes, such as those involved in Alzheimer's and Parkinson's diseases.

"That is the future hope. Right now, we feel like we are making a positive contribution towards that goal," Stanley said.

The research was supported by the National Institutes of Health. HFIR and Bio-SANS are supported by the DOE [Department of Energy] Office of Science.

Research on Huntington's Disease Is Progressing

National Institute of Neurological Disorders and Stroke

For more than a century, little sustained research was carried out on Huntington's disease. In the following selection the National Institute of Neurological Disorders and Stroke (NINDS) reviews the efforts of the past few decades. A sustained effort began in the 1960s, with support from several private foundations. Beginning in the 1970s Congress allocated funds for Huntington's disease research, and federal health agencies under the NINDS umbrella began to work on the disease in earnest. In 1993 scientists funded by the NINDS isolated the gene that causes Huntington's disease. Since then research has fanned out over a number of disciplines and approaches. Some investigators are studying the defective protein that the huntingtin gene produces, others are using advanced medical imaging techniques to peer into the brains of Huntington's patients, and still others are investigating the disease in mice and other animals. Many questions remain, but the research effort into Huntington's disease is unrelenting.

SOURCE: National Institute of Neurological Disorders and Stroke, "Huntington's Disease: Hope Through Research," August 13, 2010. Copyright © 2010 by the National Institute of Neurological Disorders and Stroke.

The NINDS is a part of the National Institutes of Health. The mission of the NINDS is to reduce the burden of neurological disease through research, grant making, and information sharing.

In 1872, the American physician George Huntington wrote about an illness that he called "an heirloom from generations away back in the dim past." He was not the first to describe the disorder, which has been traced back to the Middle Ages at least. One of its earliest names was *chorea*, which, as in "choreography," is the Greek word for dance. The term chorea describes how people affected with the disorder writhe, twist, and turn in a constant, uncontrollable dance-like motion. Later, other descriptive names evolved. "Hereditary chorea" emphasizes how the disease is passed from parent to child. "Chronic progressive chorea" stresses how symptoms of the disease worsen over time. Today, physicians commonly use the simple term Huntington's disease (HD) to describe this highly complex disorder that causes untold suffering for thousands of families.

More than 15,000 Americans have HD. At least 150,000 others have a 50 percent risk of developing the disease and thousands more of their relatives live with the possibility that they, too, might develop HD.

Until recently, scientists understood very little about HD and could only watch as the disease continued to pass from generation to generation. Families saw the disease destroy their loved ones' ability to feel, think, and move. In the last several years [before 2010], scientists working with support from the National Institute of Neurological Disorders and Stroke (NINDS) have made several breakthroughs in the area of HD research. With these advances, our understanding of the disease continues to improve. . . .

A Slow Start for Research

Although HD attracted considerable attention from scientists in the early 20th century, there was little sustained research on the disease until the late 1960s when the Committee to Combat Huntington's Disease and the Huntington's Chorea Foundation, later called the Hereditary Disease Foundation, first began to fund research and to campaign for federal funding. In 1977, Congress established the Commission for the Control of Huntington's Disease and Its Consequences, which made a series of important recommendations. Since then, Congress has provided consistent support for federal research, primarily through the National Institute of Neurological Disorders and Stroke, the government's lead agency for biomedical research on disorders of the brain and nervous system. The effort to combat HD proceeds along the following lines of inquiry, each providing important information about the disease:

Basic neurobiology. Now that the HD gene has been located, investigators in the field of neurobiology—which encompasses the anatomy, physiology, and biochemistry of the nervous system—are continuing to study the HD gene with an eye toward understanding how it causes disease in the human body.

Clinical research. Neurologists, psychologists, psychiatrists, and other investigators are improving our understanding of the symptoms and progression of the disease in patients while attempting to develop new therapeutics.

Imaging. Scientific investigations using PET [positron emission tomography] and other technologies are enabling scientists to see what the defective gene does to various structures in the brain and how it affects the body's chemistry and metabolism.

Animal models. Laboratory animals, such as mice, are being bred in the hope of duplicating the clinical features of HD and can soon be expected to help scientists learn more about the symptoms and progression of the disease.

Fetal tissue research. Investigators are implanting fetal tissue in rodents and nonhuman primates with the hope that success in this area will lead to understanding, restoring, or replacing functions typically lost by neuronal degeneration in individuals with HD.

These areas of research are slowly converging and, in the process, are yielding important clues about the gene's relentless destruction of mind and body. The NINDS supports much of this exciting work.

Working Out the Genetic Puzzle

For 10 years, scientists focused on a segment of chromosome 4 and, in 1993, finally isolated the HD gene. The process of isolating the responsible gene—motivated by

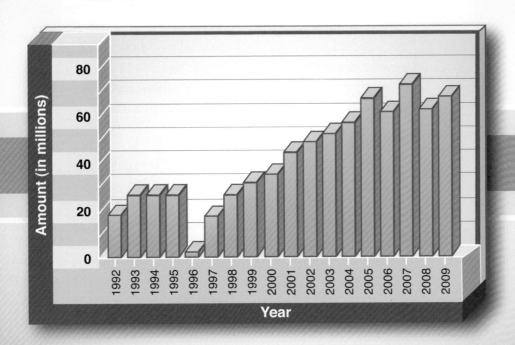

Research Funding for Huntington's Disease, 1992–2009

Taken from: Research Crossroads, "Huntington's Disease Crossroads: Funding History," www.researchcrossroads.org.

the desire to find a cure—was more difficult than antici-pated. Scientists now believe that identifying the location of the HD gene is the first step on the road to a cure.

Finding the HD gene involved an intense molecular ge-netics research effort with cooperating investigators from around the globe. In early 1993, the collaborating scientists announced they had isolated the unstable triplet repeat DNA sequence that has the HD gene. Investigators relied on the NINDS-supported Research Roster for Huntington's Disease, based at Indiana University in Indianapolis, to ac-complish this work. First started in 1979, the roster contains data on many American families with HD, provides statis-tical and demographic data to scientists, and serves as a li-aison between investigators and specific families. It provided the DNA from many families affected by HD to investigators involved in the search for the gene and was an important component in the identification of HD markers.

For several years, NINDS-supported investigators in-volved in the search for the HD gene made yearly visits to the largest known *kindred* with HD—14,000 individuals —who live on Lake Maracaibo in Venezuela. The contin-uing trips enable scientists to study inheritance patterns of several interrelated families.

A Mysterious Protein

Although scientists know that certain brain cells die in HD, the cause of their death is still unknown. Recessive diseases are usually thought to result from a gene that fails to pro-duce adequate amounts of a substance essential to normal function. This is known as a loss-of-function gene. Some dominantly inherited disorders, such as HD, are thought to involve a gene that actively interferes with the normal func-tion of the cell. This is known as a gain-of-function gene.

How does the defective HD gene cause harm? The HD gene encodes a protein—which has been named *huntingtin* —the function of which is as yet unknown. The repeated

CAG sequence in the gene causes an abnormal form of huntingtin to be made, in which the amino acid glutamine is repeated. It is the presence of this abnormal form, and not the absence of the normal form, that causes harm in HD. This explains why the disease is dominant and why two copies of the defective gene—one from both the mother and the father—do not cause a more serious case than inheritance from only one parent. With the HD gene isolated, NINDS-supported investigators are now turning their attention toward discovering the normal function of huntingtin and how the altered form causes harm. Scientists hope to reproduce, study, and correct these changes in animal models of the disease.

> **FAST FACT**
>
> The Hereditary Disease Foundation, the largest private funder of Huntington's disease research, makes grants of up to fifty thousand dollars.

Huntingtin is found everywhere in the body but only outside the cell's nucleus. Mice called "knockout mice" are bred in the laboratory to produce no huntingtin; they fail to develop past a very early embryo stage and quickly die. Huntingtin, scientists now know, is necessary for life. Investigators hope to learn why the abnormal version of the protein damages only certain parts of the brain. One theory is that cells in these parts of the brain may be supersensitive to this abnormal protein.

Tracing the Death of Cells

Although the precise cause of cell death in HD is not yet known, scientists are paying close attention to the process of genetically programmed cell death that occurs deep within the brains of individuals with HD. This process involves a complex series of interlinked events leading to cellular suicide. Related areas of investigation include:

- *Excitotoxicity.* Overstimulation of cells by natural chemicals found in the brain.
- *Defective energy metabolism.* A defect in the power plant of the cell, called *mitochondria*, where energy is produced.

- *Oxidative stress.* Normal metabolic activity in the brain that produces toxic compounds called free radicals.
- *Trophic factors.* Natural chemical substances found in the human body that may protect against cell death.

Several HD studies are aimed at understanding losses of nerve cells and *receptors* in HD. Neurons in the striatum are classified both by their size (large, medium, or small) and appearance (spiny or aspiny). Each type of neuron contains combinations of *neurotransmitters.* Scientists know that the destructive process of HD affects different subsets of neurons to varying degrees. The hallmark of HD, they are learning, is selective degeneration of medium-sized spiny neurons in the striatum. NINDS-supported studies also suggest that losses of certain types of neurons and receptors are responsible for different symptoms and stages of HD.

What do these changes look like? In spiny neurons, investigators have observed two types of changes, each affecting the nerve cells' dendrites. Dendrites, found on every nerve cell, extend out from the cell body and are responsible for receiving messages from other nerve cells. In the intermediate stages of HD, dendrites grow out of control. New, incomplete branches form and other branches become contorted. In advanced, severe stages of HD, degenerative changes cause sections of dendrites to swell, break off, or disappear altogether. Investigators believe that these alterations may be an attempt by the cell to rebuild nerve cell contacts lost early in the disease. As the new dendrites establish connections, however, they may in fact contribute to nerve cell death. Such studies give compelling, visible evidence of the progressive nature of HD and suggest that new experimental therapies must consider the state of cellular degeneration. Scientists do not yet know exactly how these changes affect subsets of nerve cells outside the striatum.

Studying HD in Mice

As more is learned about cellular degeneration in HD, investigators hope to reproduce these changes in animal models and to find a way to correct or halt the process of nerve cell death. Such models serve the scientific community in general by providing a means to test the safety of new classes of drugs in nonhuman primates. NINDS-supported scientists are currently working to develop both nonhuman primate and mouse models to investigate nerve degeneration in HD and to study the effects of excitotoxicity on nerve cells in the brain.

Investigators are working to build genetic models of HD using *transgenic mice.* To do this, scientists transfer the altered human HD gene into mouse embryos so that the animals will develop the anatomical and biological characteristics of HD. This genetic model of mouse HD will enable in-depth study of the disease and testing of new therapeutic compounds.

Another idea is to insert into mice a section of DNA containing CAG repeats in the abnormal, disease gene range. This mouse equivalent of HD could allow scientists to explore the basis of CAG instability and its role in the disease process.

Research on Fetal Tissue

A relatively new field in biomedical research involves the use of brain tissue grafts to study, and potentially treat, neurodegenerative disorders. In this technique, tissue that has degenerated is replaced with implants of fresh, fetal tissue, taken at the very early stages of development. Investigators are interested in applying brain tissue implants to HD research. Extensive animal studies will be required to learn if this technique could be of value in patients with HD.

Involving Patients in Research

Scientists are pursuing clinical studies that may one day lead to the development of new drugs or other treatments to halt the disease's progression. Examples of NINDS-supported investigations, using both asymptomatic and symptomatic individuals, include:

Genetic studies on age of onset, inheritance patterns, and markers found within families. These studies may shed additional light on how HD is passed from generation to generation.

Studies of cognition, intelligence, and movement. Studies of abnormal eye movements, both horizontal and vertical, and tests of patients' skills in a number of learning, memory, neuropsychological, and motor tasks may serve to identify when the various symptoms of HD appear and to characterize their range and severity.

Clinical trials of drugs. Testing of various drugs may lead to new treatments and at the same time improve our understanding of the disease process in HD. Classes of drugs being tested include those that control symptoms, slow the rate of progression of HD, and block effects of excitotoxins, and those that might correct or replace other metabolic defects contributing to the development and progression of HD.

Medical Imaging Helps Investigators

NINDS-supported scientists are using positron emission tomography (PET) to learn how the gene affects the chemical systems of the body. PET visualizes metabolic or chemical abnormalities in the body, and investigators hope to ascertain if PET scans can reveal any abnormalities that signal HD. Investigators conducting HD research are also using PET to characterize neurons that have died and chemicals that are depleted in parts of the brain affected by HD.

Like PET, a form of magnetic resonance imaging (MRI) called functional MRI can measure increases or decreases in certain brain chemicals thought to play a key role in HD. Functional MRI studies are also helping in-

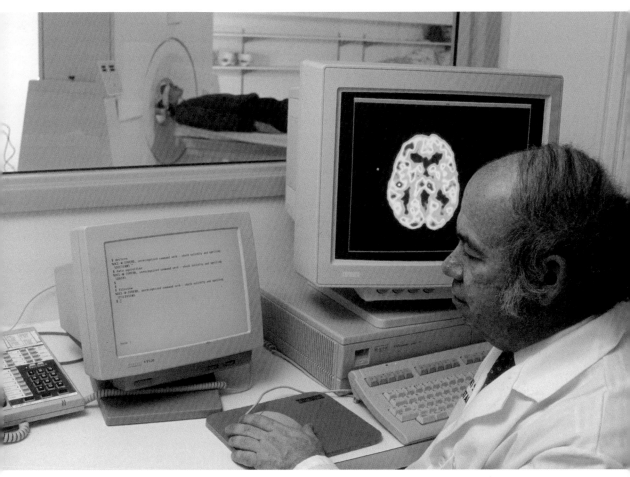

vestigators understand how HD kills neurons in different regions of the brain.

Imaging technologies allow investigators to view changes in the volume and structures of the brain and to pinpoint when these changes occur in HD. Scientists know that in brains affected by HD, the basal ganglia, cortex, and ventricles all show atrophy or other alterations.

The Human Factor

In order to conduct HD research, investigators require samples of tissue or blood from families with HD. Access to individuals with HD and their families may be difficult

Huntington's disease research includes positron-emission tomography brain scans (pictured) and other imaging techniques that enable scientists to analyze the effects of defective genes on various structures in the brain and how they affect the body's chemistry. (© Hank Morgan/Photo Researchers, Inc.)

however, because families with HD are often scattered across the country or around the world. A research project may need individuals of a particular age or gender or from a certain geographic area. Some scientists need only statistical data while others may require a sample of blood, urine, or skin from family members. All of these factors complicate the task of finding volunteers. . . . NINDS-supported efforts bring together families with HD, voluntary health agencies, and scientists in an effort to advance science and speed a cure.

CHAPTER 2

Controversies Concerning Huntington's Disease

There Are Good Reasons to Know Whether One Has the Gene for Huntington's Disease

Eryn Brown

Even though a genetic test for Huntington's disease has become available, many of those at risk have avoided finding out their status. As the following selection makes clear, however, there can be important benefits to getting tested. Eryn Brown tells the story of a brother and sister whose family was plagued by the gene that causes the disease. The siblings struggled with the decision to get tested, but both decided to go ahead for the sake of their families. Without the information, they realized, they could not make good decisions about the future. Brown is a science and medicine writer for the *Los Angeles Times*.

Anew study in the journal *Pediatrics* show[s] that many parents would choose genetic testing for their kids if such screening might show the risks of heart disease, cancer and other disorders that the kids face. The study noted that many of the parents who said

Photo on previous page. Ongoing genetic research may hold the key to defeating Huntington's disease. (© Richard T. Nowitz/Photo Researchers, Inc.)

SOURCE: Eryn Brown, "Genetic Testing: One Family Faces Down Huntington's Disease," *Los Angeles Times*, April 19, 2011. Copyright © 2011 by the Los Angeles Times. All rights reserved. Reproduced by permission.

they were interested in testing believed their results would be reassuring.

But going through genetic testing can be an emotional roller coaster, even when the news is ultimately good, affecting people beyond the patient getting the test. Families, and their genes, are interconnected.

"People don't understand how far-reaching this information is," said Jim Nelson of Los Angeles. "It's hard to own the information by yourself."

A Fatal Family History

Nelson knows first hand. His father and paternal grandmother both died of Huntington's disease, a degenerative and fatal ailment of the brain that is passed down from parent to child. Children of people with Huntington's disease have a 50% chance of carrying the gene themselves—and if they have the gene they will develop the disease, given time.

Of Nelson's four siblings two were known to have the gene for Huntington's; Nelson's sister Debbie is already in the throes of the disease. At age 55, she must use a wheelchair and has trouble speaking and swallowing, among other difficulties. "It is all too horrible to even try to explain," Nelson said. A third sibling died of cancer at 33 and was never tested.

Learning you will develop Huntington's is devastating. For many years, Nelson and another sister, Laurie Dixon of Placerville, Calif., had decided that they wouldn't get tested, waiting until signs of the disease showed up to find out if they were carriers. Recently both changed their minds. But it wasn't easy, Nelson wrote in an email:

"Watching Huntington's flow down through your family tree is devastating. You are always wondering who is going to have to bear this horrible burden next. The

> **FAST FACT**
>
> Genetic counselors can help individuals make difficult decisions about testing. The American Board of Genetic Counseling certifies genetic counselors in the United States.

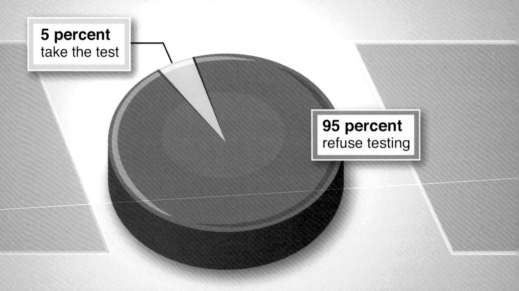

Testing for Huntington's Disease

A minority of people at risk for Huntington's disease choose to be genetically tested for the disease.

5 percent
take the test

95 percent
refuse testing

Taken from: Francis O. Walker, "Huntington's Disease," *Lancet*, January 20, 2007.

mothers in our family look at their children every day with great joy, as well as a fear that can sometimes be crippling. When you trip over something, especially when it's your own two feet, a bolt of panic jolts you, as you question the possible onset of Huntington's."

"You want to know, and you don't want to know," he said.

Seeking Anonymity

Nelson eventually went to UCLA [the University of California at Los Angeles] and was tested under an assumed name and ID, to avoid insurance complications. "Waiting for the results was 'HELL!!!'" he wrote. He felt guilty that he waited to tell his sister, with whom he speaks often, that he'd had the test.

For her part, Dixon was sort of forced into examining her DNA: She decided to go through with testing when her son, David, who wanted to start a family, made a screening appointment of his own to find out if he carried the Huntington's gene. If David was a carrier, he and his wife Brittany had decided, they would not have biological kids. But their right to know their own genetic destiny posed a problem for Dixon. She wasn't sure she was ready to know about hers. "If he had [the gene], it would mean I absolutely had it," she said.

Dixon asked her son to postpone his test so she could think it over, and then she secretly went to UCLA. In the

People with a family history of Huntington's disease should be tested to determine whether they carry the defective gene, thus enabling them to make informed decisions about their future.
(© Mehau Kulyk/ Photo Researchers, Inc.)

end both she and Nelson got good news: They didn't have the Huntington's gene.

A Tidal Wave of Emotions

From Nelson: "When I went in for my follow up appointment, and found out I was 'clean,' I could not believe the flood of emotions. I was on the floor in tears. I couldn't even leave the building, because I was shaking. I left the office, but had to go back and sit down. I couldn't get in a car, so I had to walk around. I went to a neighborhood store, and the cashier asked me how I was doing. I said 'fine,' and started bawling my eyes out. She must have thought I just left the psych ward at UCLA. I tripped—and laughed for the first time, instead of going into a panic.

"To this day, I still cry when I think of some aspect of this disease. I am crying now."

Dixon, who got her results some time later than Nelson, presented the good news to David and Brittany as a Christmas present. They are now planning to start a family—one that won't live under the shadow of Huntington's disease.

Many People Do Not Want to Know or Reveal a Diagnosis of Huntington's Disease

Laura Spinney

Huntington's disease is thought to be rare, but that could be a re-flection of the stigma and denial surrounding the condition. In the fol-lowing selection Laura Spinney discusses the reasons why people tend to conceal a diagnosis of the deadly disease, shield their chil-dren from the news, or simply refuse to be tested. According to Spin-ney, far from being a rare disease, Huntington's might be relatively commonplace, hidden from view by those who fear discrimination in employment or marriage or those who are concerned about being re-fused health insurance. Additionally, she says, many people who are at risk simply do not want to know whether they are in fact fated to die from an incurable disease. Spinney is a science reporter for the British newspaper the *Guardian*.

O n June, 30, 2010, an All Party Parliamentary Group on Huntington's disease will be launched in the UK. The group's first task will be to inves-tigate the true prevalence of Huntington's disease, because a discrepancy exists between the prevalence estimate that the UK government has been working with and that suggested by the number of people seeking advice from the UK-based Huntington's Disease Association.

"The figure that is generally reported is seven symptomatic people per 100000", says Michael Rawlins, chairman of the National Institute for Health and Clinical Excellence for England and Wales. "The Huntington's Disease Association has 6376 [symptomatic people] on its books in England, which works out at 12.4 per 100000." In other words, if these figures accurately reflect the UK situation, the prevalence of Huntington's disease has been underestimated by 80%. Because the figures from the Huntington's Disease Association are themselves almost certainly an underestimate, Rawlins says it is reasonable to suggest that Huntington's disease might be twice as prevalent in the UK as it was previously thought to be.

Stigma Stymies Counts

The prevalence figures from the Huntington's Disease Association have yet to be validated, and Rawlins—along with Sarah Tabrizi of University College London's Institute of Neurology, London, UK, who leads a research programme on Huntington's disease, and Stephen Evans, an epidemiologist at the London School of Hygiene and Tropical Medicine—is now designing a study to do just that. Their research will involve combing general practice databases for diagnoses of Huntington's disease, validating those diagnoses, and then working out the prevalence of Huntington's disease in the UK. Rawlins is confident that they will have a revised prevalence estimate by the end of 2010. However, measuring prevalence is not easy, he warns, particularly for a disease that has been so stigmatised.

Huntington's disease is a fatal, genetic neurodegenerative disorder that causes involuntary movements, emotional disturbance, and progressive cognitive loss over

10–20 years. Every child of an affected parent has a 50% chance of inheriting the disease gene, and carriers of the gene will definitely develop the disease although, in most cases, not until the third or fourth decade of life. By then, many patients have already had children, and so these children have to witness the decline that awaits one in two of them.

There are several reasons why Huntington's disease prevalence might have been underestimated. Although the course of the disease is fairly characteristic and therefore misdiagnosis is relatively rare, it does happen, particularly in less common cases in which psychiatric symptoms precede the movement disorder. The introduction of a genetic test in the early 1990s reduced the risk of misdiagnosis; however, many people with a family history of Huntington's

Genetic testing for Huntington's is important because every child of an affected parent has a 50 percent chance of inheriting the gene for the disease. (© Jan Halaska/ Photo Researchers, Inc.)

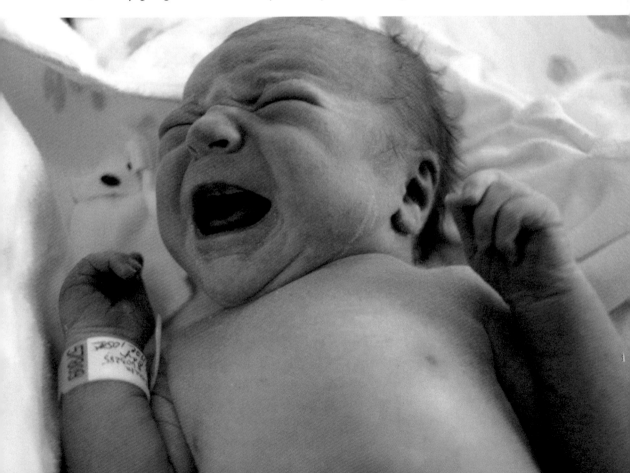

disease prefer not to know if they are carriers, and those who have been diagnosed may hide their diagnosis for as long as they can. In addition, in the UK, doctors are not legally required to enter the cause of death on a death certificate, and so not all deaths from Huntington's disease are recorded.

Incentives to Hide the Disease

Nancy Wexler, a geneticist and neuropsychologist at Columbia University in New York, USA, who led the team that located the gene that causes Huntington's disease, is delighted that the prevalence of Huntington's disease will finally be investigated properly. If the prevalence has been underestimated in the UK, she says, it has probably been underestimated elsewhere. In fact, she says, the prevalence usually quoted for the USA—ten symptomatic individuals per 100000—might be even more of an underestimate than in the UK because Americans have an added incentive to hide their at-risk status owing to insurance companies' practice of refusing health coverage to people with pre-existing conditions.

Although last March [2010], US President Barack Obama signed a law prohibiting insurance companies from denying coverage to children with such conditions, and the protection will be extended to adults in 2014, Huntington's disease remains stigmatised. Wexler—whose mother died of the disease—believes this is in part because of the history of compulsory sterilisation of Huntington's disease carriers in the USA, which was first proposed around 1910 by US eugenicist Charles Davenport, and which continued into the second half of the 20th century. "To understand the problems in getting at the true prevalence", says Wexler, "you have to understand the shadows people are walking out of."

Cath Stanley, who runs the Huntington's Disease Association's care services for England and Wales, says there is likely to be a feedback effect if the higher prevalence figures are confirmed: knowing their condition is more common than they thought might encourage more patients to come forward. Armed with the new figures, the charity plans to campaign for more National Health Service (NHS) resources to be allocated to Huntington's disease, on the principle that the NHS guarantees equality of treatment to all, and patients with Huntington's disease are being underserved because of the underestimated prevalence. The quality of care that is currently on offer is patchy, says Stanley: "If you have a specialist, multidisciplinary Huntington's disease clinic in your area, you probably get very good medical care", she says. "If you don't, that might not be the case."

Future Victims May Be Hidden

The revised prevalence figures will be important for several reasons. First, if the prevalence of a disease as relatively easy to diagnose as Huntington's disease has been underestimated, then the prevalence of disorders for which there is no genetic test and for which diagnosis is less clear-cut, such as Alzheimer's disease and Parkinson's disease, might have been underestimated too. Second, because Huntington's disease often does not manifest until middle age, the number of patients who have symptoms at any given time is just the tip of the iceberg. Carriers who have yet to develop symptoms are not included in the prevalence figures, yet there are more of them: "The rule of thumb is that the number of presymptomatic people in a population is roughly twice the number of symptomatic", says Rawlins.

The presymptomatic population will expand dramatically if the increased prevalence figures are confirmed. In the early stages of Huntington's disease, before the disease manifests, whole-brain volume is significantly reduced and there are differences in regional grey and white matter.

Genetic Testing for Serious Diseases

In a 2010 survey, 1,000 adults aged 18 and older were asked: "Would you consider having your genetic profile analyzed to learn if you are susceptible to diseases such as Alzheimer's, cancer, and diabetes?"

Answer	All	Age 18–49	50+
Yes	29%	29%	28%
No	70%	70%	69%
Don't know/ No response	2%	1%	3%

Taken from: *AARP Bulletin*, "Poll: Genetic Testing," September 1, 2010. www.aarp.org/health/medical-research/info-08-2010/poll_genetic_testing.html.

Therefore, one goal of pharmaceutical companies is to develop neuroprotective treatments that carriers could take presymptomatically to prevent damage to the brain from ever reaching the threshold at which symptoms emerge.

The CHDI [Cure Huntington's Disease Initiative] Foundation, a US-based, not-for-profit research organisation, plans to launch clinical trials for two potential treatments for Huntington's disease within the next 2 years. "If they're effective for manifest Huntington's disease, we'll wind the window back and see how effective they are in premanifest populations", says Simon Noble, the foundation's director of communications. He would also like to see research designed to quantify the number of presymptomatic patients.

Huntington's May Not Remain Rare

The USA was the first country to introduce legislation to induce pharmaceutical companies to develop orphan drugs—that is, drugs for rare diseases, such as Huntington's disease—with the 1983 US Orphan Drugs Act. The European Union followed suit in 2000. The incentives these laws put in place included simplified licensing procedures for candidate drugs and extended patent protection. However, the prevalence threshold for defining a rare disease varies widely, from 11 cases per 100000 in Australia, to 75 per 100000 in the USA.

If the UK prevalence figures suggested by the Huntington's Disease Association also applied to Australia, which is by no means a given since Huntington's disease prevalence varies geographically, then Huntington's disease would stop being classed as a rare disease in Australia. According to Christopher McCabe, a health economist at Sheffield University in the UK, this reclassification wouldn't necessarily affect a pharmaceutical company's decision to invest in research on Huntington's disease, because most companies plan globally and Huntington's disease is likely to remain rare in most parts of the world. But it might influence where companies decided to launch any newly licensed treatments: "They'll launch first in the places where they have orphan drug status, because it's easier", he says. This happened in the case of interferon beta for multiple sclerosis, for example, which was marketed first in the USA, where it was considered an orphan drug, and only later in Europe, where it was not.

In the European Union, a rare disease is defined as one that is life-threatening or chronically debilitating, with a

> **FAST FACT**
>
> One study in the journal *Neurology* found that the death rate for Huntington's patients would be 80 percent higher if other causes of death exacerbated by Huntington's disease were taken into account.

prevalence of 50 or fewer cases per 100000. Therefore, even if the revised prevalence of Huntington's disease in the UK is twice as high as that with which the UK government is currently working, the disease will continue to be defined as rare. Patients could now begin to see a difference, however, as the new All Party Parliamentary Group strives to ensure that they have access to the health care and political representation that is due to them.

Genetically Engineered Monkeys May Lead to a Better Understanding of Huntington's Disease

Quinn Eastman

In the following selection Quinn Eastman tells of the dilemma facing researchers at the Yerkes National Primate Research Center and Emory University's Woodruff Health Sciences Center. In 2008 they published breakthrough research on the use of rhesus monkeys genetically altered for the study of Huntington's disease. Monkeys are genetically much closer to humans than more commonly used mice, but as scientists learned, inducing Huntington's disease in them is difficult and carries risks. During the first round of experiments, many of the monkeys died shortly after birth. Researchers plan to try inducing a less severe form of the disease in hopes that the next round of monkeys will survive longer and provide scientists with insights about how to detect and ultimately treat the disease. Despite the difficulties, scientists say they need to work with monkeys because they cannot further advance their knowledge working only with mice. Eastman is a medical journalist who writes about basic and clinical biomedical research at Emory University.

SOURCE: Quinn Eastman, "A First in Monkey Models," *Emory Health*, Winter 2009. Copyright © 2009 by Emory Health. All rights reserved. Reproduced by permission.

After creating the first model of a human neurodegenerative disease in rhesus monkeys, [veterinary neuroresearcher] Anthony Chan and his colleagues at the Yerkes National Primate Research Center and Emory's Department of Human Genetics are thinking hard about where to go next with their powerful transgenic technology.

Last spring [2009], *Nature* published their research on rhesus monkeys engineered to develop an aggressive form of Huntington's disease. Chan reports that his team is already at work developing a more subtle simulation of Huntington's. In addition, he is starting to think about adding other genes to monkeys, which could provide insights into diseases ranging from diabetes to cancer.

But Chan says caution is in order because monkeys take longer to mature than laboratory mice. "We have to think strategically, because there's a huge commitment involved in caring for and monitoring the animals," he says.

Researchers routinely insert human genes into mice to simulate human diseases. However, successfully performing the same feat in monkeys required technology that Chan has been refining since his graduate school days in the 1990s.

Mice Are Imperfect Models

With mice, scientists inject foreign DNA directly into a just-fertilized egg using a fine needle, a dependable enough approach in small animals. However, the reliability of this approach drops off with monkeys and large animals such as cows and pigs, Chan says.

His alternative combines a viral vehicle for the DNA and a technique used by infertility specialists. First, the scientists usher the foreign DNA into a monkey egg cell by cloaking it with a lentivirus. In this case, the best results come when the target egg is reached before fertilization. Then the investigators perform in vitro fertilization

—injecting sperm directly into the egg—and transfer the early embryos into surrogate mothers. The longer life spans of monkeys make translating the transgenic model of Huntington's disease from mice a multistep process.

In people with Huntington's, a single gene carries a mutation that lengthens one section of the genetic code, so that three letters (CAG) are repeated dozens of times. Mutant proteins produced as a result of this coding error clump together inside brain cells. Huntington's patients gradually lose control of their speech, movements, and even swallowing. The longer the repeated region, the fiercer the disease, scientists have found.

A researcher draws blood from a rhesus monkey. Because mice are imperfect subjects for Huntington's research, an aggressive form of the disease is developed in rhesus monkeys for study by researchers. (© Peter Menzel/Photo Researchers, Inc.)

Monkeys Are Soon Devastated

In an early round of developing a Huntington's model in monkeys, the Yerkes researchers introduced genes with 84

CAGs. Some of the animals survived for less than a day because of respiratory difficulties. One monkey with a milder form of the disease displayed involuntary movements sporadically at one week of age, but eventually the symptoms grew much worse.

Chan hypothesizes that because monkeys take longer to mature than mice—three years until puberty versus six weeks—the toxic protein has more time to build up in cells. Accordingly, in the next group of monkeys, the researchers will use shorter CAG repeats (73) and introduce other differences in hopes of simulating a gradual onset of Huntington's, like that in humans.

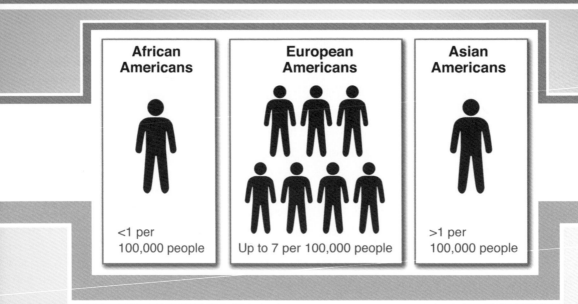

Human Genetic Variation Affects the Incidence of Huntington's Disease

African Americans

<1 per 100,000 people

European Americans

Up to 7 per 100,000 people

Asian Americans

>1 per 100,000 people

Taken from: Francis O. Walker, "Huntington's Disease," *Lancet*, January 20, 2007.

The goal, Chan says, is to monitor the animals through brain scans and regular samples of blood and cerebrospinal fluid, with an eye out for genes or proteins that look like early warning signs of damage to the brain. "With a suitable marker, we may be able to test treatments for safety and confirm efficacy as a critical step on the path between other animal models and people," he says.

Transgenic primate models with other human diseases such as Alzheimer's or fragile X syndrome, the most common form of inherited mental retardation, are likely to come next. Chan's colleague at Yerkes and Alzheimer's expert Lary Walker says that a primate model could illuminate areas of research that continue to puzzle his field, such as why monkeys don't seem to be harmed by the protein plaques that develop in their brains and are characteristic of Alzheimer's. "Essentially, we've hit the wall as far as progress with the mouse model," Walker says.

FAST FACT

A 2007 study showed that the gene defect that causes Huntington's disease could reproduce many facets of the disease in mice.

Monkeys Should Not Be Used for Research

Gill Langley

In the following selection scientist Gill Langley, a leading opponent of animal testing, reviews the growing call for a prohibition on such research and the reasons behind the call. Chief among these is the recognition that the closer to human an animal is, the more its capacity to suffer is like our own. Writing on behalf of the British Union for the Abolition of Vivisection (BUAV), Langley rejects anthropocentrism, the belief that humans have greater moral worth than other animals, which seeks to justify inflicting suffering on animals to benefit humans through advances in research. Langley is a former animal researcher who now campaigns against the practice for the BUAV and other organizations. The BUAV is a London-based nonprofit organization that campaigns peacefully to end experiments on animals.

In political terms, several countries have taken steps to prevent experiments on our closest primate cousins. New Zealand, Great Britain (since 1998), Sweden, Austria and the Netherlands have already introduced bans on the use of great apes (chimpanzees, bonobos, gorillas and orangutans) in research and testing.

Sweden's 2003 regulations banned research on great apes and gibbons; only non-invasive behavioural studies are permitted. And following a unanimous vote of the Austrian Upper Chamber in December 2005, all apes in Austria, including all eight species of gibbons, are now protected from research unless conducted in the interests of the individual animal.

In 2002, the Belgian Minister responsible for animal welfare announced that Belgium would be working towards a ban on all primate experiments. Furthermore, the British Animal Procedures Committee's remit includes "... *how to minimize, and eventually eliminate, primate use and suffering*".

The European Commission, in response to growing criticism, commissioned an analysis of primate use throughout the European Union. The subsequent report acknowledged, in considerable detail, the cognitive complexity of these animals and their capacity to suffer in laboratories.

Like Humans, They Suffer

According to Britain's Nuffield Council on Bioethics, primates are used in many areas of neurobiology because their brains share structural and functional features with ours, but *"While this similarity has scientific advantages, it poses some difficult ethical problems, because of an increased likelihood that primates experience pain and suffering in ways that are similar to humans"*.

The Boyd Group, comprising researchers (including primate experts), research-funding agencies, animal welfarists and philosophers, has called for a global prohibition on the use of all great apes in research and testing. The Group also agreed that experiments on other primates

Several countries and a number of organizations have called for banning the use of humans' primate cousins as research subjects. (© Nathan Benn/Alamy)

should require very strong justification, while some members supported a total ban on the use of monkeys as well as apes. . . .

At the Fifth World Congress on Alternatives and Animal Use in the Life Sciences in August 2005, [renowned British primatologist] Jane Goodall was joined by 57 individuals and organisations from 19 different countries in signing a resolution calling for an end to the use of all primates in biomedical research and testing.

Despite the growing weight of opinion against primate experiments, there is no evidence that they are decreasing, either in Europe or the USA. In fact, the most recent European Union statistics revealed a 14% increase in the number of primates used. Thus it seems that the views of primate researchers are diverging rapidly from those of the public on whose behalf they conduct their experiments.

All Primates Are Sentient

The key issue with experimentation on primates, as for all animals, is the capacity to suffer. If an animal does not consciously experience pain, for example because it lacks the faculties to generate feelings of suffering and distress (i.e. it is not sentient), then we need not be concerned about causing individual harm (although there may be other concerns).

The vertebrate animals used in research and testing are sentient. This is accepted throughout the European Union as evidenced by the legally-binding protocol of 1997 annexed to the Treaty of Amsterdam, by which acknowledgement of animal sentience—the *"ability to experience pleasure and suffering"*—was written into EU [European Union] law. Animal sentience is also recognised in the wording of European Directive 86/609/EEC as well as the UK Animals (Scientific Procedures) Act 1986, which regulate scientific procedures on animals with the capacity to experience *"pain, suffering, distress or lasting harm"*. The UK Act also covers one invertebrate species. *Octopus vulgaris*, for which the scientific case for sentience has been considered sufficiently compelling.

The fact that sentient animals feel pain and distress is sufficient reason, on moral grounds, to avoid inflicting them. However in the case of experimentation, it is often argued that the potential benefits to humans justify keeping animals in unnatural and highly confined conditions and causing them pain, suffering and distress. We disagree with this anthropocentric viewpoint.

In addition to pain sensation, issues of mental complexity also impact on the moral status of animals. There is persuasive evidence that many animals—certainly mammals, probably birds and possibly other species—have thoughts, feelings, memories and intentions.

> **FAST FACT**
>
> According to People for the Ethical Treatment of Animals, no type of animal experiment is illegal in the United States.

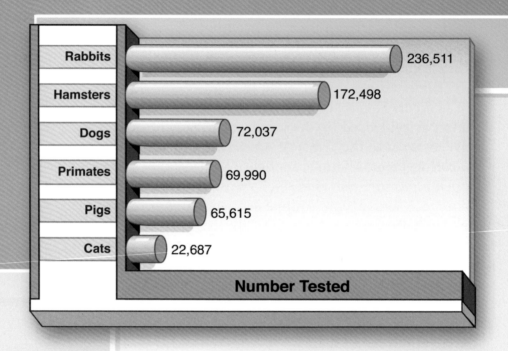

Top Animal Species Used in US Laboratory Experiments (Excluding Rats and Mice)

Species	Number Tested
Rabbits	236,511
Hamsters	172,498
Dogs	72,037
Primates	69,990
Pigs	65,615
Cats	22,687

Taken from: Stop Animal Exploitation Now!, "Animal Experimentation in the United States," 2009. www.all-creatures.org/saen/fact-anex-jun09.html.

Modern studies in ethology, genetics, neurophysiology, neuropharmacology and psychology have shown that there is no abrupt discontinuity between humans and all other primates in terms of ability to feel pain, distress and suffering; or in their morally-relevant cognitive, social and emotional faculties. Rather, there is a spectrum of capacities throughout the animal kingdom (including humans), with considerable overlap between species. This biological continuity offers no support for moral positions that discriminate absolutely between all humans and all other animals.

As Britain's Animal Procedures Committee report on the laboratory use of primates acknowledged: " . . . *there are serious ethical and animal welfare concerns regarding the use of primates in experiments and considerable public disquiet with regard to such use. These concerns are also likely to increase as more is discovered about their advanced cognitive faculties, complex behavioural and social needs, and the difficulties of satisfying these in a laboratory environment*".

The Moral Status of Primates

Many primates share with humans the ability to remember past events, to have desires, to anticipate and plan for future events, to communicate, form concepts and have complex emotional and social experiences, as this chapter describes. These attributes are morally significant because they show that other primates are harmed not only by physical pain, but also by mental and emotional distress—such as is caused by a barren environment, frustration, restraint or social isolation and the presence, or anticipation, of something fearful or painful.

Globally, the Netherlands, New Zealand, Great Britain, Sweden and Austria have already introduced some form of prohibition on the use of great apes in laboratories. In the case of Sweden, gibbons are also protected from invasive experiments. In other countries such as Germany, Italy and Norway, great apes have not been used in research and testing for some years. However, most importantly, in the USA there are currently more than a thousand chimpanzees in research facilities, and with the publication of the chimpanzee genome, there are plans to increase research efforts using these animals. . . .

Experiments on great apes continue in the USA, with the possibility of an increase in the near future. . . . There is no biological rationale for distinguishing between the moral status of humans and all other primates.

Marijuana Is a Legitimate Treatment for Huntington's Disease

Adi Jaffe

Medical marijuana has been prescribed for various conditions, but it is not often associated with the treatment of Huntington's disease. In the following selection, however, researcher Adi Jaffe touts its potential to relieve the symptoms of Huntington's disease. Citing a study carried out in Madrid, Jaffe says the results suggest that the active ingredient in marijuana, tetrahydrocannabinol, or THC, may relieve symptoms and perhaps even slow the progression of the disease. Jaffe is an addiction researcher at the University of California at Los Angeles.

We recognize that saying we have an addiction problem is not the same as saying we have a drug use problem and that just because some people abuse substances (or belief systems) doesn't mean that these have no actual value when not abused. Enter this recent paper on [the brain's] CB1 receptors, THC

SOURCE: Adi Jaffe, "THC for Huntington's Disease? CB1 Receptors Important for More than Drug Use," *Psychology Today*, February 25, 2011.

[tetrahydrocannabinol, an active ingredient in marijuana], and Huntington's Disease.

Those of you who haven't been reading [this column] may not be familiar with my comparison of the cognitive (or mental) impulsivity associated with substance use disorders and the physical "impulsivity" common to Huntington's Disease (HD) patients. To make a long story short—both of these dysfunctions have to do with the striatum, a brain area responsible for inhibiting and controlling unwanted brain output (as in thoughts or actions). When this area starts malfunctioning, everything goes awry. When it comes to HD, "goes awry" doesn't really do the disorder justice. Patients with a progressive form of the condition end up flailing their limbs in a manner that's been coined the "Huntington Dance," a euphemism if I ever heard one. This motor flailing is closely followed by severe cognitive impairments and a premature death. Not a pretty story.

Public Support for Medical Marijuana

Regardless of what you think about the personal, nonmedical use of marijuana, do you think doctors should or should not be allowed to prescribe marijuana for medical purposes to treat their patients?

Date	Should	Should not	No opinion
1/15/10	81	18	1

Percent

Taken from: *Washington Post*/ABC News poll, January 12–15, 2010.

The Role of the Receptors

In the striatum, CB1 receptors (the most common cannabinoid receptors and the main target for THC) are very important in this mechanism of inhibiting output. In fact, there's some evidence that their activation is important in saving cells from dying in cases of over excitation, an idea we'll return to shortly. It's important to note that Huntington's patients and animal models of the disease have been shown to have reduced levels of CB1 receptors in this area.

A group of researchers in Madrid wanted to examine what exactly the role of this reduced cannabinoid receptors was in the development of Huntington's Disease. The researchers created transgenic mice that expressed both the human version of the HD gene (called huntingtin) and reduced levels of CB1 receptors (we'll call these the combined-type mice). Using a battery of tests that are supposed to assess motor coordination, exploration, and strength, the researchers compared these mice with mice expressing only the huntingtin gene.

The results were pretty clear: Having reduced CB1 receptors made HD symptoms appear four weeks earlier in the combined-type mice when compared with the HD mice and the disease symptoms also progressed much more quickly. The CB1 deficit was also associated with a greater level of neuron loss in the striatum and a whole mess of other problems with neuron structure. It was clear that these mice were suffering due to the increased absence of cannabinoid receptors.

As a therapeutic experiment, the researchers then tried to give THC to the huntingtin mice (not the combined-type this time, that wouldn't do much since they don't have CB1 receptors . . .). The reasoning went that if losing

CB1 receptors made things worse then maybe activating those receptors more strongly in HD mice would make their symptoms better—and it worked! Giving HD mice THC improved their motor function, slowed the disease symptom progression, and improved the volume of their striatum.

A deeper look into the mechanism of this revealed that as mentioned earlier, the activation of CB1 receptors by THC apparently served a protective role and helped the HD mice delay, or reduce, the extent of neuron loss in their striatum that was the cause for all their Huntington's Disease symptoms.

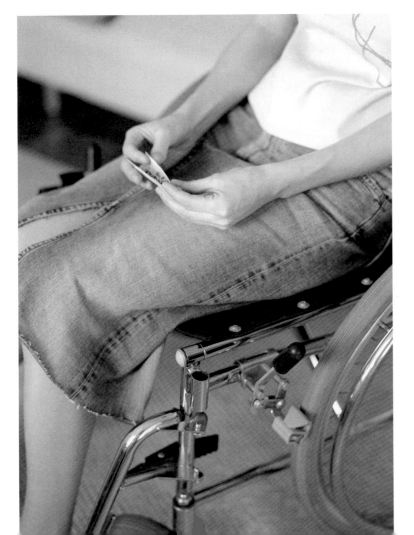

Experiments on mice in Madrid, Spain, have revealed that tetrahydrocannabinol, the active ingredient in marijuana, may relieve symptoms and slow the progression of Huntington's disease. (© Lee Powers/Photo Researchers, Inc.)

THC Shows Real Promise

The idea that THC can be used to relieve disease symptoms isn't a new thing—Glaucoma, HIV, and cancer patients have all benefited from the use of CB1 agonists whether in the form of marijuana leaves or a pharmacologically similar product. Nevertheless, the idea of using THC or other CB1 agonists for the treatment of HD is pretty new. There have been a small handful of studies but only one well-constructed experiment that used a placebo-controlled crossover design, which yielded some positive results. The results of this study suggest that THC and other CB1 compounds may not only be able to improve symptoms in already symptomatic HD patients, but also slow down the progression of such a devastating disease. Good news all around and a great use of THC as far as I'm concerned.

Medical Marijuana Is Not a Legitimate Medical Treatment

Charles Lane

Controversy surrounds the use of marijuana as a legal treatment for various ailments while it remains illegal as a recreational drug. In the following selection Charles Lane scoffs at the idea that marijuana is a legitimate medicine. He says he does not necessarily oppose its legalization as a recreational drug similar to alcohol, but the notion that there is such a thing as "medical marijuana" is, Lane declares, "hokum." Scientific evidence for its therapeutic benefits, he says, is entirely lacking. He lambastes the Barack Obama administration for backing off from the enforcement of federal drug laws when it comes to medical marijuana. In particular, he is incensed at the failure to require that marijuana be treated like other medical drugs, with proponents forced to demonstrate its safety and efficacy to the Food and Drug Administration. Lane is a *Washington Post* editorial writer who specializes in economic policy, financial issues, and trade but occasionally takes on health care issues as well.

SOURCE: Charles Lane, "Medical Marijuana Is an Insult to Our Intelligence," *PostPartisan* (blog), October 20, 2009. www.washingtonpost.com. Copyright © 2009 by the Washington Post. All rights reserved. Reproduced by permission.

The Justice Department [DOJ] says it's backing off the prosecution of people who smoke pot or sell it in compliance with state laws that permit "medical marijuana." Attorney General Eric Holder says "it will not be a priority to use federal resources to prosecute patients with serious illnesses or their caregivers." Party hardy! I mean—let the healing begin!

I don't think the federal government should be spending a whole lot of time on small-time druggies, and I'm undecided about legalizing pot, which enjoys 44 percent support among the general public, according to a recent poll. Recreational use is not the wisest thing—and if my 12-year-old son is reading this, that means you!—but it's no more harmful than other drugs (e.g., alcohol) and impossible to eradicate. On the other hand, I worry it's a gateway to harder stuff. So I think we probably should have an open debate about decriminalization.

Get Real About Decriminalization

But it should be a real debate, about real decriminalization, and not clouded—pardon the expression—by hokum about "medical marijuana." To the extent it puts the attorney general's imprimatur on the notion that people are getting pot from "caregivers" to deal "with serious illnesses"—as opposed to growing their own or flocking to "dispensaries" just to get high—the Justice Department's move is not so constructive.

I do not deny that for some people, including some terminal cancer patients and pain-wracked AIDS sufferers, marijuana is a blessed relief. Let 'em smoke, I say, just as the Justice Department has usually ignored such cases since long before Holder spoke up. But if you believe there is any scientific evidence that smoked marijuana has the multiplicity of therapeutic uses that advocates claim— well, I've got a bag of oregano I'd like to sell you.

Usually, drugs have to pass exacting testing by the Food and Drug Administration [FDA] before they go on the market. There's a good reason for this: we don't want people spending money on products that might be ineffective or actually harmful. In California and elsewhere, however, snake oil—sorry, "medical marijuana"—got on the market via a different route: popular referendum. The pot for sale in dispensaries is subject to none of the purity controls that actual pharmaceutical drugs must meet. Indeed, the new DOJ policy essentially recognizes a gray market for pot, leaving these supposedly seriously ill people at the mercy of their dealers—I mean caregivers—with respect to quality and efficacy.

What other substances should we handle this way? Cocaine? Laetrile [a cancer drug of unproven effectiveness]? Didn't President [Barack] Obama just sign a bill authorizing the FDA to regulate the nicotine content of tobacco? And I thought he promised to "restore science to its rightful place."

A medical marijuana dispensary in Los Angeles, California, is shown here. Calling the purity of medical marijuana into question, opponents of its use point out that the drug is not subject to the governmental controls and regulations imposed on pharmaceutical companies. (© wonderlandstock/ Alamy)

No Prescription Needed

Under California's law, you don't even need a prescription to get pot (which would admittedly have been a problem, since the U.S. Drug Enforcement [Administration] controls who gets a prescription pad, and not many doctors would use theirs to prescribe an illegal drug). All it takes is a "written or oral recommendation" from a physician.

A few years ago, a California woman called Angel Raich took her defense of medical pot all the way to the Supreme Court. She lost on the legal issue, which had nothing to do with the medical effectiveness of pot. Along the way, though, she claimed that she was suffering from "life-threatening" weight loss (due to a chronic inability to hold down food, which her doctors could not explain). She also cited chronic pain from scoliosis, temporomandibular joint dysfunction, bruxism, endometriosis, headache, rotator cuff syndrome, uterine fibroids, and Schwannoma [a tumor of peripheral nerves]. The Latin names of these latter conditions might have snowed some judges, but physicians recognized each of them as a common, non-life-threatening problem for which conventional treatments were available. Raich listed a cornucopia of potent drugs, from Vicodin to Methadone, that she had tried previously and gotten no satisfaction.

> **FAST FACT**
>
> According to the National Organization for the Reform of Marijuana Laws, a survey of California medical marijuana clinics found that the leading uses of the drug are to relieve pain and insomnia.

This is not an isolated instance. According to a survey by NORML [the National Organization for the Reform of Marijuana Laws], the pro- "medical marijuana" organization, which can be expected to emphasize the desperate health of users, only 22 percent of California medical marijuana users suffer from AIDS-related disease. Most of the rest have more subjective maladies such as "chronic pain" or "mood disorders."

Raich's physician was Frank Lucido, a well-known Berkeley doctor and pro-pot activist—he also makes money as an expert witness on "medical marijuana"—whose Web site boasts that he was "investigated by the Medical Practices Board of California for cannabis evaluation practices in 2003, and fully exonerated." The case involved his recommendation of marijuana to treat attention deficit disorder in a 16-year-old boy, but, as I say, he was fully exonerated.

Where's the Science?

In a brilliant article on this subject in the *Hastings Center Report*, a bioethics journal, lawyer and anesthesiologist

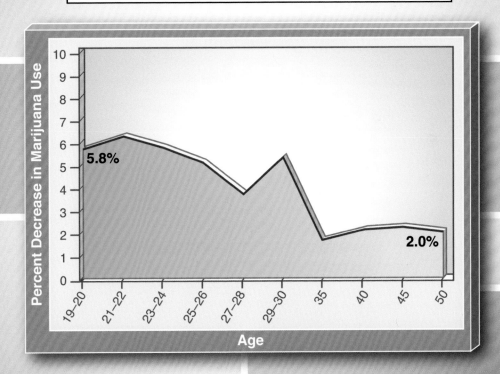

Marijuana Use Decreases with Age

Peter J. Cohen noted that "medical marijuana" groups have been notably passive about demanding FDA testing and approval for this purported elixir. Instead, they took their case to the people. As Cohen argued, this is no way to make health policy: "Medical marijuana," he wrote, should be "subjected to the same scientific scrutiny as any drug proposed for use in medical therapy, rather than made legal for medical use by popular will." The "medical marijuana" movement may not be a threat to our civilization, but it is an insult to our intelligence.

CHAPTER 3

Personal Experiences with Huntington's Disease

Getting Tested for Huntington's Disease

Smiling Sarah

The decision to get tested requires great courage on the part of those who know they may have Huntington's disease. A positive result is a death sentence from which there is no appeal. In the following selection a woman known as "Smiling Sara" tells of her decision and its aftermath. Having made up her mind to get tested, she found that it is no easy thing to achieve. She had to save up money for the cost of the test and then endure a waiting list. After many months she got her test and then had to cope with the consequences of finding out that she is indeed fated to get the disease. Still, she shows a remarkably determined and cheerful attitude in the face of a bleak forecast. The Huntington's Disease Lighthouse is a website dedicated to supporting individuals and families affected by Huntington's disease.

I had known since I was a kid that Grandma had had HD [Huntington's disease], and that I had a 25% chance of getting it, but felt that as long as my Mom was healthy,

Photo on previous page. A Huntington's disease patient receives a soothing hand massage at a Duluth, Minnesota, health center that offers restorative aid to deal with the disease. (© AP Images/Duluth News Tribune/Bob King)

SOURCE: Smiling Sara, "Still Coping with My Test Results a Year Later," *Huntington's Disease Lighthouse*, April 12, 2011. www.hdlf.org. Copyright © 2011 by Huntington's Disease Lighthouse. All rights reserved. Reproduced by permission.

we were all safe. I never worried about it until the day that someone outside my family said "Do you think your Mom might have what your Grandma had?" I instantly realized they were right, and from that day I could not get it out of my head.

Besides worrying about Mom's health, the 50/50 chance that I would have this hit me like a ton of bricks. I hit the internet hard, and found lots of info that only cemented my conclusion that Mom must have it, plus I found out about genetic testing and some of the clinical trials & studies going on.

A Months-Long Wait

I had no doubt that I needed to get that genetic test, then decide what further action to take. By the time I researched a testing place, saved the money, and got on the wait list it was 5 months. I couldn't stand the waiting, but besides giving me time to see how sure I was, it did also give me time to get all my insurance in order. I figured I had a 50% chance of being negative and feeling so much better. But that if I were positive I would take that OK too, somehow. I wanted to get my own results behind me, whatever they were, so I could focus better on Mom. Plus if I were positive, I wanted to participate in whatever trials/studies were available, take any supplements that are suspected to help, and live life to the fullest.

My husband supported testing as being MY decision, but I could tell he did NOT want to know. Still, what was I to do? I was obsessing anyway; may as well rip the band-aid off, and see what's underneath, then let the true healing begin if needed.

Sleepless Nights

Still, since I do not have symptoms (besides a little tendency to obsess—which anyone can have), we WERE a little surprised that it was positive. We got the news on a Friday, and hadn't slept well leading up to it, but sleeping that weekend was even worse. I really wished I would have gotten a prescription for stress-relief/sleeping, but I would have a glass of wine before bed instead. I added NyQuil the night before my results, which I only share as ammunition for others to ask for something safer than NyQuil + wine.

After the results, I worried how differently my husband would look at me, knowing I had the gene, and he'd likely eventually be my care-taker. I started to wonder how we could modify our house for wheelchair accessibility. I wondered if we'd gotten ENOUGH insurance, and read all the fine print. I started thinking about what instructions to leave as an Advanced Care Directive. I had a constant pit in my stomach for 1–2 weeks, just dreading the future. (And again, no meds, also no follow-up call from my testing center). I went to work but was really not mentally there. I had only told my husband and 3 of our closest friends in addition to the lighthouse forum, but you can only talk about it so much, anyway.

I tried to find enjoyable distractions. We started making wine at home. Thankfully it was springtime, so I started some seeds for my garden, and spent time outside when it was nice enough. I did further research and ordered my supplements. I found a study to sign up for. I've always been a runner, but running was now really helping with my stress. . . .

I forced myself to visit my Mom—because I realized I would want someone to do that for me. But I went without my husband most of the time, not wanting him to see her and think that's going to be me someday (bad enough that I was thinking that).

Keeping Busy as a Volunteer

We had also recently found a church to join, after really not going for years. I threw myself into volunteer projects, including some that put me around others who were certainly worse off than myself (had immediate health issues

+ financial issues). Now I manage some of those projects a) because I like helping people; b) because I CAN; and c) never hurts to have good deeds under your belt.

A friend of mine was getting married, across the country; invitations came right after my test. I had just gone to visit the previous year and it would have been financially smart to stay home from the wedding. But I'd told myself I was going to live life to the fullest so I went—and was so glad that I did!

I also find myself making more effort to go along with any fun suggestions that my husband or friends have. Not being careless with money, but prioritizing a fun experience like a concert, over some new clothes. . . .

I think about HD multiple times/day. I still often get that pit in my stomach even though I really do think there's a lot of hope for treatments/virtual-cure that will drastically change what it means to have HD—soon!

A Positive Outlook

The testing process was by far the most stressful thing I've ever been through, and the fresh positive result was even worse. It was probably about 2 months before my stress level was back to the pre-testing-process level (still high). I guess it is significantly lower today, over a year later; but it's taken a lot of effort to get here. I AM back to living life, trying to live it to the fullest. And I count my blessings, including the 30+ years I was able to not worry about HD, and everything I am able to enjoy today.

HD is not coming for me tomorrow. I may have 5 "good" years or 65, or somewhere in between. HD may be cured before it significantly affects my health. Anything else could end my life on any given day. So I'm making sure that my life includes people and activities that I enjoy, and hopefully also leaves some good effect on others.

> **FAST FACT**
>
> According to the *American Journal of Medical Genetics*, a survey of at-risk patients who refused to be tested for Huntington's disease found that two leading reasons for their reluctance were the difficulty of facing the risk to their children if the test were positive and the knowledge that no cure is available.

A Huntington's Patient Shares His Sense of Loss

Phil Hardt

Huntington's disease disables long before it kills. In the following selection Phil Hardt describes his struggles working as the symptoms of Huntington's set in. He suffered from memory lapses and physical difficulties. His sense of balance was suspect. Before long the disease compromised his ability to drive. His boss surprised him by proving sympathetic and reassigning him to a desk job, but eventually even that became untenable. Hardt writes movingly about the emotional aftermath of his helplessness as well as the support that sustains him. Although Huntington's disease ended his career, Hardt has continued to do volunteer work in Prescott, Arizona.

My problems started with me not being able to remember simple instructions from my boss. There were times when I felt off balance at work and would have to lean against something for a while. There were also times when I would look directly at a part number and it not register. I don't know if I was actually seeing it but it wasn't registering or what. When this happened I found it best just to stop what I was doing and do something else for a while. Once I returned to the original task the next day I would be able to find the "missing" part.

I became a great liar and I hated it. I would say stuff like I forgot about the meeting or about talking with another person, or it was next to do on my list when in reality I wouldn't have the foggiest idea what my boss was talking about. I resorted to carrying 3 x 5 index cards in my pocket with copious notes written on them to get by for a while but they were only good as long as I remembered them.

At this time I was setting up inventory control systems on our production floor. First I would organize data on my computer to determine how big the storage racks needed to be by each part number and then actually move all the inventory out of the main warehouse into my new "store."

Losing Mental Abilities

At the same time I was moonlighting at the local community college and teaching spreadsheets, word processing, and Windows 95/NT. I had to quit teaching because I couldn't even answer questions on material I had just lectured on. I also had to resort to reading the material right out of the book. I didn't like doing this either.

My driving woes started when I forgot how to shift. (I know, when was the last time you even thought about what you do when you shift!) In addition I also found myself getting lost while driving and resorted to leaving early for work and staying late so I wouldn't get frustrated if it happened.

The worst thing to happen to me was I began running red lights. I would see it but not even remember to stop. I was very concerned about hurting someone else or incurring a huge lawsuit that my family couldn't afford.

We bought an automatic so I wouldn't have to manually shift but then the next thing I couldn't do was judge the distance to safely stop when the cars in front of me would put on their brakes. This meant lots of screeching stops or actually rear-ending the car in front.

Needless-to-say, I finally gave up the car keys. One of the blessings was that one of my fellow co-workers heard about my problems and asked me to car pool with him. I told him that I wouldn't be able to "share" the driving but wanted to pay him for the weeks that I should have been driving. He refused and became a very true friend who still corresponds with me.

The Word Gets Out

I was petrified to tell my boss but one of my co-workers did it for me because he said I was unsafe to be around moving equipment and machinery because of my jerks, memory and balance problems. I had heard that they would probably demote me and then when I finally couldn't work anymore, I would get 60% of the lower salary for my long-term disability.

To my surprise, after my boss called me in he was totally sympathetic, arranged for me to do a desk job AND keep my present salary. He said he knew that I would be able to also keep my same medical/dental once I got in 10 years of service and that would only be 8 months away.

He was another blessing. The new desk job reduced some of my stress and allowed me to make the time required.

My oldest two daughters both decided to get married within a month of each other (I think to make it easier on us). When my boss found out about this he called me in and handed me an envelope. I had no idea what was in it but broke down and cried when I opened it and found a

> **FAST FACT**
>
> Huntington's disease typically becomes apparent between the ages of thirty and forty-five, although onset may occur as early as age two.

check for almost $9,000 from some expensed chemicals that he had gotten permission to give the refund to us because he knew marriages were expensive.

Life Without Work

When I got closer to 10 years I took a neuro-psych test and flunked it so my psychologist recommended it was time to quit. After quitting, ALL of my physical problems quickly ended for about a year. I never knew how much stress I was actually coping with!

Since being home I've had to cope mostly with emotional problems such as severe depression, feelings of worthlessness, etc. I've noticed that it's almost like I don't have any emotions now. I know it sounds funny but everything that I loved and cherished before, I don't seem to have any feelings for now, or the feelings/emotions are greatly reduced. This scares me. I know some of the things I've done would never, never, never have happened before but now that they have, I don't feel any remorse or sadness for them.

I'm not sure who I am anymore, etc. It's almost like when I'm doing hurtful things I don't realize it (or maybe it's just not caring anymore) until a long time afterwards and then I don't feel sorry for what I've done and am virtually emotionless. Thank goodness I have a very loving and forgiving wife—my greatest blessing.

Remembering is becoming harder and I've also started having a hard time spelling, finding words to describe things, or even saying them without going: "M m m m m meredith" for Meredith, etc. I have also started pausing at weird spots when I speak.

Thanks for all the love and concern from everyone.

Finding the Will to Live with Huntington's Disease

Charlotte Raven

A diagnosis of Huntington's disease presents a bleak prospect. Although research continues, there is no cure and little treatment. In the following selection Charlotte Raven shares an intimate journey to the edge of suicide and back, following her discovery that she has the disease in her genes. Raven tested positive shortly after the birth of her daughter. She considered the examples of others who have suffered and those who have chosen to end their lives. Finally, she traveled to Venezuela to visit a ramshackle town full of Huntington's disease sufferers. There the determination of a doomed mother changed Raven's mind about the validity of choosing to end her life. Raven is an author and journalist who was born in Manchester, England.

In 2006, 18 months after the birth of my baby, I tested positive for Huntington's disease. The nurse who delivered the news hugged me consolingly and left me with my husband and a mug of sweet tea to cry. In the

SOURCE: Charlotte Raven, "Charlotte Raven: Should I Take My Own Life?," *Guardian*, (Manchester, UK) January 16, 2010. Copyright © 2010 by The Guardian. All rights reserved. Reproduced by permission.

days that followed, I began to realise why so few of the people at risk of inheriting this incurable neurodegenerative disorder chose to find out.

This incuriosity had seemed to me irresponsible. Having discovered the previous year that my father had the disease, I had been offered a test that would tell me for certain if I, too, had inherited the gene. In the months of debate I'd had with my husband about whether to take the test, I'd always been on the side of enlightenment. I calculated that the trauma of finding out would be offset by the satisfaction of being able to make informed decisions about my life.

I thought taking the test would be like finding out the weather before you go on holiday.

If the outlook was gloomy, at least I'd know what to pack. In reality, it was more like finding out there was a bomb on the plane when you were already airborne. I felt impotent and envious of the uninformed majority. I wished I didn't know. . . .

Fear of Being an Awful Mother

At home with a toddler, the prospect of losing my newly discovered maternal feelings seemed particularly hard. The typical HD personality is demanding and unempathic —most unmaternal. I feared becoming an obstruction to be navigated round: a succubus draining life from the family host. I couldn't stand the thought of my daughter being scared of me. I pictured her dawdling at the top of the street on her way home from school, putting off the moment she would have to confront an irascible and unpredictable parent. I feared I might set fire to the house with her in it, like [legendary folksinger] Woody Guthrie's HD-affected mother. Or parade in front of her school friends in my underwear.

Having tested positive for HD, I was told it was inevitable that I would develop the disease at some point—

but that it was not possible to know when. HD typically strikes in midlife. A fortunate few like my father suffer no symptoms until as late as their 60s, but for most it begins in their late 30s to mid-40s. I am 40 years old.

Frustratingly, some friends and family recast this certainty as a probability. "You might not get it," they would say, offering half-remembered quotes from articles about the neuroprotective benefits of fish oil. I began to feel like the only evolutionist in a room full of creationists. I understand why they do it. A hereditary illness for which there is no cure is a challenge to our sense of ourselves as self-determining entities. Having invested so much in the fantasy that we are authors of our fate, we would rather credit ourselves with the power to generate miracles than accept the incontrovertible evidence to the contrary.

The most up to date research on fish oil suggests that it does nothing to alleviate the symptoms or slow the disease's inexorable progress. Knowing this, my dad still takes 1,000mg a day.

Although fish oil is recommended by some practitioners to alleviate Huntington's symptoms or to slow the progress of the disease, research has turned up no evidence of such benefits.
(© **Photo Researchers, Inc.**)

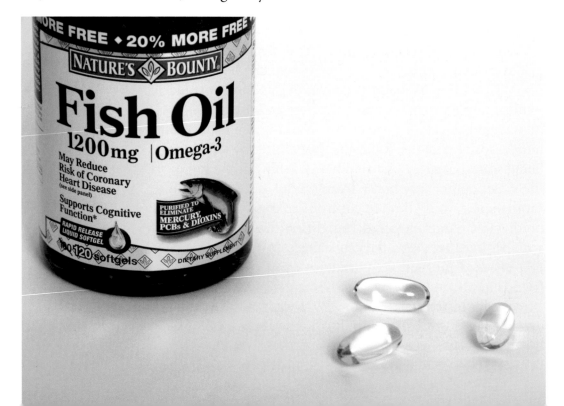

My first suicidal thought was a kind of epiphany—like Batman figuring out his escape from the Joker's death trap. It seemed very "me" to choose death over self-delusion. Ah ha, I thought. For the first time since the diagnosis, I slept through the night.

I was shocked to read the figures for HD-related suicide. One in four people with the illness tries to kill themself. I was surprised it wasn't more. Rationally, you would have thought that everyone with the condition would realise the futility of continuing. Yet three-quarters of sufferers carried on. Why? Had they been duped by family members into believing they were not as far gone as they felt? Or were they falling for some misplaced belief in the sanctity of life? Their decision to cast the destruction of their identity and descent into madness as a challenge rather than a disaster seemed irrational, yet weirdly threatening.

Considering Self-Destruction

I felt I had to argue them out of it. My mind clicked into gear, issuing bullet points to back up the case for self-destruction:

If my cat had HD, I wouldn't make it carry on, but would get the vet to put it out of its misery.

- Without autonomy and the capacity for self-determination, life is meaningless. Merely existing isn't enough.
- Dependency is degrading.
- Suffering is pointless. The religionists' belief that it is spiritually instructive, and therefore an essential part of life, is dangerous and reactionary.

When Nancy Wexler's mother attempted suicide, her father discovered her and saved her life. His daughter says he later felt that saving his wife's life had been a "terrible mistake". He'd acted out of instinct, and subsequently regretted not respecting her wishes. If he had, she might have been spared the miserable years that followed.

I feared my husband would do the same. His opposition to my arguments in favour of killing myself when the time came was instinctual rather than intellectual. He couldn't offer any supporting evidence for his sense that a suffering, angry and dependent wife was better than a dead one.

He was right about one thing, though. My belief that he wouldn't be able to bear watching me suffer *was*, he said, a projection. *I* couldn't bear watching me suffer. I had already found myself wondering every time I misplaced my keys or failed to locate my phone charger whether this was the beginning of my decline.

I wanted to set a date. The first stages of the disease are often characterised by denial. Sufferers can spend the early years convinced there is nothing wrong. I feared that by the time I became fully aware of how bad I had got, I would no longer be physically capable of enacting my own death. I decided a pre-emptive strike would be necessary.

I pictured a room in the Chelsea hotel and me, still young and unscathed by the muscular spasms that contort the faces of HD sufferers. I would still be capable of grasping and expressing the poignancy of my situation. My suicide note would be pitched at posterity. I would administer a fatal dose of heroin and that would be that. The idea of going during the pre-symptomatic period had a lot to recommend it. I'd be able to "author" my death in the way I authored my wedding, ensuring that it was poetic and resonant. More importantly, I'd never be tempted to blog my descent into incoherence. Did the people journaling endlessly on all those HD websites never, I wondered, talk or think of anything else? Their devotion to their disease seemed drone-like, and I cleaved towards the pro-euthanasia lobby, sensing they were more my type.

Seeking Role Models

[Conservative columnist] Dominic Lawson has observed the right-to-die lobby comprises "powerful people" who are used to exerting control over their lives, and I suppose I thought of myself as one of them. I'd never had a normal job and found it hard to cope with people telling me what to do. My opinions were my own, developed without reference to God, convention or morality. I considered myself intellectually autonomous (as if such a thing were possible).

I identified heavily with the portrayal of PSP (progressive supranuclear palsy) sufferer Anne Turner in the BBC's well-intentioned drama *A Short Stay in Switzerland*, which tackled the increasingly fashionable theme of euthanasia. Confronted with her neurological malaise, Turner was steely and determined to enact the rationally arrived at decision to die: "You know what has to be done and you just do it."

Dynamic decision-makers such as Turner regard a loss of control over their lives as a fate worse than death. They perceive patient-hood as degrading. I perceived it as a form of oppression. HD seemed like the worst kind of corporate boss, defining my agenda and limiting my capacity for self-expression. Resisting gave me a buzz I hadn't felt since my youth. I was fighting for my rights!

Having regained control over her life by her decision to die, Turner becomes calm. I felt the same sense of inner peace, convinced I would be doing the right thing for my family. The film's deathbed scene at Dignitas[1] showed the family grieving healthily. Experiencing closure, you sense they will recover quickly—and so it proves.

According to Derek Humphry, author of a seminal 1991 euthanasia textbook, "The closure in a case of accelerated, date-fixed dying is more effective and poignant because everybody concerned knows in advance that the patient will be gone at a pre-ordained time." I wanted to give my family the same gift.

---

1. Dignitas is a Swiss-based assisted suicide organization.

Humphry also promised better days ahead. With the matter settled, I'd be free to make the most of the time remaining. But only if I laid my plans carefully. Meticulous forward planning was necessary for "self-deliverance with certainty".

A Letter to Her Daughter

With this in mind, I began composing a letter to my daughter. The act would be impossible to account for when there was nothing observably wrong. At risk herself (she cannot choose to take the test to see if she has inherited the gene until she turns 18), she would be terrified about what was to come. Rather than rush, I realised I'd have to wait until midway through the illness. It was important to write now, while I was still making sense. . . .

The next few weeks were spent adjudicating methods. Overdosing on heroin in the Chelsea hotel seemed hackneyed, on reflection.

The Dignitas route was expensive but effective. Three thousand pounds [about $5,000] would buy three consultations and a lethal dose of the drug popularly considered to be the least physically and emotionally traumatic way to go. I guessed this was what [British Parliament member] Baroness Warnock and other proponents of assisted dying meant when they talked about "easeful death". In their accounts, suicide was a gorgeous Saturday morning lie-in, not a violent rupture.

The success rate was 100%, though it was clear that not everyone "went" at the same pace. The process took anything from 15 minutes to several hours to complete. . . .

A Trip to See HD Victims

Apart from my dad, I'd never seen anyone with HD. His affected relatives were all kept under wraps. I became fas-

> **FAST FACT**
>
> A study of Huntington's disease patients in Massachusetts found that those over age fifty have more than eight times the risk of suicide as the general population.

cinated by Wexler's report of a community of HD sufferers in Venezuela where, through an accident of history, HD has become endemic. Her account of the inhabitants of the fishing villages on the shores of Lake Maracaibo was shocking and compelling, and eventually I decided to go there myself. En route to Barranquitas, I worried my curiosity might prove ill-advised. An article in *Business Week* said the town was "like something out of the Twilight Zone".

On arrival, I was surprised how much of the scene was recognisable from Wexler's 20-year-old accounts. There was still no sanitation or running water. The shacks where most of the victims lived looked no more commodious. Here were the kids with their prematurely furrowed brows. And here was Lake Maracaibo, glinting ironically.

In one compound I was introduced to a family of eight. They described life with their HD-affected relative. For the past few years, Mariela had been aggressive, fighting her family and shouting at the kids. She was no longer herself, but a cipher of the illness. From her sister Marisela's account, it was clear she is in the later stages of what they call "el mal"—the evil. I was shocked to discover that she was seven months pregnant, but not surprised to learn that her symptoms worsened during pregnancy. I felt a stab of concern for her unborn child.

A local clinic offers sterilisation to patients with el mal. The doctor there says she has terrible trouble persuading women to have the operation. Mariela refused, even though she already had three children. How irresponsible, I thought.

According to her sister, Mariela often threatens to throw herself into the lake. Her raging seems to support the pro-suicide lobby's contention that life without self-determination is intolerable. The repulsive image of Mariela gasping for breath in the toxic waters of this polluted lake, as her body's reflexes conflict with her will, haunted me for weeks. . . .

Ties to Others Trump Suicide

Marisela said that when she goes to work she worries about her sister. She described her relief, every time she comes home, on finding her alive. My expectation that I'd detect a note of ambivalence in the relief was misplaced. The trauma and tedium of life spent caring for this doppelganger is, for Marisela, preferable to the alternative. Whenever it happened, if it ever did, her sister's suicide would play as self-destruction rather than self-deliverance.

I had never thought of suicide as violent or vile, and no wonder—our preferred methods are designed to obscure this painful reality. Suicide consumers have been sold a chimera of a "peaceful" end. The suppression of our suffocation responses has made it possible for us to think of suicide as an idea rather than a physical process. I now see that suicide isn't a modest proposal but a very immodest one.

This realisation was most unwelcome, like finding out your lover's true nature. I was still in love with the idea of easeful death, and yet the knowledge—this dark apprehension of the truth—couldn't be put aside. It may have played a part in Mariela's unwillingness to carry out her threats, but it wasn't the whole story. With a sinking heart, I apprehended the rest.

"Does she still love her children?"

"Yes."

"Do they know it?"

"Yes." She gestured up towards a tree. "When she's swinging here in the hammock with the kids playing underneath, everything is OK."

One peculiarity of HD is that it leaves intact the sufferers' ability to love their family. This is both the best thing about the illness and the worst. It means sufferers are likely to choose life, with all that this implies—and explains why Mariela has chosen a decade of terrible suffering over death.

Maternal love pins Mariela to the shore, defiantly producing children. I no longer feel she is irresponsible to refuse sterilisation. Mariela is landlocked, I realise, and so am I. The lake's redemptive promise cannot be fulfilled. Suicide is a fantasy. Loving my daughter, I am doomed to live....

Back home, I told my husband he was right. The case for carrying on can't be argued. Suicide is rhetoric. Life is life.

GLOSSARY

anxiety
A feeling of apprehension and fear that can result in physical symptoms such as rapid heartbeat, sweating, and nervous twitches.

chorea
Constant, rapid, complex body movements that resemble a dance but are involuntary.

chromosome
A well-defined segment of DNA that contains a set of genes.

cognitive
Having to do with mental processes such as being aware, knowing, thinking, learning, and judging.

depression
A mental illness that involves a loss of energy, motivation, and hope.

DNA (deoxyribonucleic acid)
The molecule that serves as the main carrier of genetic information. It is composed of base pairs of nucleic acids organized into genes bundled into chromosomes. Together they form a code for forming proteins.

dystonia
Involuntary movement and prolonged muscle contractions that result in twisting, cramps, and immobility. It may affect the entire body or only an isolated area.

gene
A discrete segment of DNA that forms the basic unit of heredity. If functional, it codes for a certain function or trait (often in combination with other genes).

genetic disease
A disease caused by an abnormality in one or more genes in a person's genome.

genetic testing
Tests performed to determine whether a genetic disease or the risk of one is present.

heredity
The transmission of traits via genes from parents to their offspring.

PERSPECTIVES ON DISEASES AND DISORDERS

huntingtin	The gene that, when it has an excess of CAG nucleotides, gives rise to Huntington's disease. Also name of the protein that is malformed by the genetic abnormality.
mutation	A random change in the code of DNA. Among the causes of mutations are ionizing radiation, harsh chemicals, and viruses.
neurology	A specialty within medicine concerned with the diagnosis and treatment of disorders of the brain and nervous system.
nucleotide	A single unit in a DNA chain, consisting of a phosphate, sugar, and a single "letter" in the DNA "alphabet." In Huntington's disease three nucleotides spelling out CAG repeat too many times.
onset	The point at which a disease makes itself apparent through symptoms.
progressive	A disease that becomes increasingly worse in scope or severity.
striatum	A part of the basal ganglia of the brain that is often atrophied by Huntington's disease.
trait	A genetically determined physical or behavioral characteristic of an organism.
twitching	Involuntary contractions of muscle fibers that result in movement of facial features or limbs.

CHRONOLOGY

circa 1500	Swiss physician Paracelsus describes a set of symptoms as "chorea," meaning a kind of dance.
1636	English doctor Thomas Sydenham attempts to classify various kinds of chorea-causing diseases.
1842	A letter in physician Robley Duglinson's periodical *Practice of Medicine* seems to describe the specific malady that would later become known as Huntington's disease.
1846	American doctor Charles Gorman observes that a malady typified by uncontrollable shaking appears to cluster in certain geographic regions.
1860	Norwegian physician Johan Christian Lund produces an early description of the disease.
1872	American doctor George Huntington produces the first thorough description of the disease that bears his name, first in a lecture and later in a medical publication.
1893	William Osler, a British physician who settled in North America, cofounds Johns Hopkins School of Medicine and helps raise awareness of Huntington's disease.
1911	Charles Davenport, head of the new genetics laboratory at Cold Springs Harbor, New York, identifies Huntington's as a genetic disease.
1932	American psychiatrist Percy Vessie publishes a paper that traces the origins of Huntington's disease (perhaps unreliably) to a seventeenth-century village in East Anglia, England.
1953	Francis Crick and James Watson discover the structure of DNA, opening the way to unraveling the mystery of Huntington's disease.

1967 Famed folksinger Woody Guthrie dies after a long battle with Huntington's disease.

1983 The US–Venezuela Huntington's Disease Collaborative Research Project discovers the approximate location of the gene responsible for the disease.

1992 A researcher finds that DNA nucleotide repeats of CAG determine the threshold and severity of Huntington's disease.

1993 Researchers isolate the precise gene responsible for Huntington's disease on chromosome 4.

2000 A line of gene-altered lab mice is bred to develop Huntington's disease for studies of treatments.

2001 Mayo Clinic researchers discover that failed DNA repair is a causative factor in Huntington's disease.

2011 Scientists discover a blood-borne biomarker for Huntington's disease, making diagnosis easier.

ORGANIZATIONS TO CONTACT

The editors have compiled the following list of organizations concerned with the issues debated in this book. The descriptions are derived from materials provided by the organizations. All have publications or information available for interested readers. The list was compiled on the date of publication of the present volume; the information provided here may change. Be aware that many organizations take several weeks or longer to respond to inquiries, so allow as much time as possible.

American Academy of Neurology (AAN)
1080 Montreal Ave.
Saint Paul, MN 55116
(651) 695-1940
e-mail:
info@aan.com
website:
www.aan.com

The AAN is a medical specialty society established to advance the art and science of neurology in order to promote the best possible care for patients with neurological disorders.

Centers for Disease Control and Prevention (CDC)
1600 Clifton Rd.
Atlanta, GA 30333
(800) 232-4636
fax: (770) 488-4760
e-mail: cdcinfo@cdc
.gov
website: http:/cdc.gov

The federal centers are the nation's leaders in efforts to prevent and control diseases. They conduct research and advise other government agencies and the public.

Hereditary Disease Foundation
3960 Broadway
6th Fl.
New York, NY 10032
(212) 928-2121
fax: (212) 928-2172
e-mail: cures@hd
foundation.org
website: www.hd
foundation.org

This foundation is dedicated to curing Huntington's disease and other hereditary conditions. A description of the protocols involved in testing for those at risk and not symptomatic and other research news is available at its site.

Huntington Society of Canada (HSC)
151 Frederick St.
Ste. 400
Kitchener, ON
N2H 2M2
(519) 749-7063
fax: (519) 749-8965
e-mail: info@hunting
tonsociety.ca
website: www.hunting
tonsociety.ca
/english/index.asp

Based in Canada, the HSC is a national network of volunteers and professionals who have banded together to fight against Huntington's disease since 1973.

Huntington Study Group
University of
Rochester
1351 Mt. Hope Ave.
Ste. 223
Rochester, NY 14620
(800) 487-7671
website: www.hunt
ington-study
-group.org

The Huntington Study Group is a nonprofit group of physicians and other health care providers from medical centers in the United States, Canada, Europe, and Australia, experienced in the care of Huntington's patients and dedicated to clinical research of Huntington's disease.

Huntington's Disease Society of America (HDSA)
505 Eighth Ave.
Ste. 902
New York, NY 10018
(212) 242-1968
(800) 345-4372
fax: (212) 239-3430
e-mail: hdsainfo@
hdsa.org
website: www.hdsa
.org

The HDSA is dedicated to finding a cure for Huntington's disease while providing support and services for those living with the disease, as well as their families. The society promotes and supports both clinical and basic Huntington's research, aids families in coping with the multifaceted problems presented by the disease, and educates families, the public, and health care professionals about Huntington's disease.

Mayo Clinic
200 First St. SW
Rochester, MN 55905
(507) 284-2511
fax: (507) 284-0161
website: www.mayo
clinic.org

The Mayo Clinic is a not-for-profit medical center that diagnoses and treats complex medical problems. The Mayo Clinic maintains a thorough website for the public with comprehensive information on Huntington's disease.

National Institute of Neurological Disorders and Stroke (NINDS)
PO Box 5801
Bethesda, MD 20824
(800) 352-9424 or
(301) 496-5751
e-mail: www.ninds
.nih.gov/contact_us
.htm
website: www.ninds
.nih.gov

The NINDS is part of the National Institutes of Health. Its mission is to support and conduct research on the normal structure and function of the nervous system as well as the causes, prevention, diagnosis, and treatment of more than six hundred nervous system disorders. Among these is Huntington's disease.

FOR FURTHER READING

Books Gillian Bates, Peter Harper, and Lesley Jones, eds., *Huntington's Disease*. New York: Oxford University Press, 2002.

Stanley Fields, *Genetic Twists of Fate*. Cambridge, MA: MIT Press, 2010.

Susan Folstein, *Huntington's Disease: A Disorder of Families*. Baltimore: Johns Hopkins University Press, 1989.

Alison Gray, *Genes & Generations: Living with Huntington's Disease*. Wellington, New Zealand: Huntington's Disease Association, 1995.

Duncan Kyle, *The Dancing Men*. Glasgow, Scotland: Fontana Collins, 1985.

Donald C. Lo and Robert E. Hughes, eds., *Neurobiology of Huntington's Disease*. Boca Raton, FL: CRC, 2011.

Oliver Quarrell, ed., *Juvenile Huntington's Disease*. New York: Oxford University Press, 2009.

Sandy Sulaiman, *Learning to Live with Huntington's Disease: One Family's Story*. Philadelphia: Jessica Kingsley, 2007.

Alice Wexler, *Mapping Fate: A Memoir of Family, Risk and Genetic Research*. Berkeley and Los Angeles: University of California Press, 1996.

Alice Wexler, *The Woman Who Walked into the Sea: Huntington's and the Making of a Genetic Disease*. New Haven, CT: Yale University Press, 2008.

Internet Sources

Rick Alan, "Huntington's Disease," NYU Medical Center, February 14, 2007. www.med.nyu.edu/patientcare/library/article .html?ChunkIID=11772.

Nick Bascom, "Biomarker for Huntington's Disease Identified," *ScienceNews*, October 4, 2011. www.sciencenews.org/view /generic/id/334911/title/Biomarker_for_Huntington%E2%80% 99s_disease_identified.

Maria Cheng, "UK May Have Many More Cases of Huntington's," *Omaha (NE) World Herald*, June 29, 2010. www.omaha.com/article/20100629/AP08/306299764/section/go 03.

HealthDay News, "Huntington's Disease Linked to High Brain Cholesterol," *Washington Post*, December 8, 2006. www.wash ingtonpost.com/wp-dyn/content/article/2006/12/08/AR2006 120800873.html.

Tina Hesman, "Huntington's Disease Protein May Have an Accomplice," *US News & World Report*, June 5, 2009. www .usnews.com/science/articles/2009/06/05/huntingtons-disease -protein-may-have-an-accomplice.

Journal of Clinical Investigation, "New Insight into the Cellular Defects in Huntington's Disease," ScienceDaily, October 10, 2011. www.sciencedaily.com/releases/2011/10/111010122142 .htm.

Lund University, "New Discovery Explains Weight Problems in Huntington's Disease," ScienceDaily, April 6, 2011. www.science daily.com/releases/2011/04/110406132018.htm.

Medical News Today, "In Mouse Model of Huntington's Disease, Melatonin Found to Delay Onset, Reduce Deaths," October 11, 2011. www.medicalnewstoday.com/releases/235850.php.

Frank Mickaideit, "Huntington's Survivors Fight Disease," *Orange County (CA) Register*, October 6, 2011. www .ocregister.com/articles/huntington-320798-lisa-family.html.

Michael Orth, "Gene Silencing Takes a Targeted Step Forward," HD Buzz, October 7, 2011. http://hdbuzz.net/52.

Eribeth Penaranda, Angel Garcia, and Lisa Montgomery, "It Wasn't Witchcraft—It Was Huntington Disease!," *Journal of the American Board of Family Medicine*, January 1, 2011. www.jabfm.org/content/24/1/115.full.

Reuters, "First Drug Approved for Huntington's Chorea," *New York Times*, April 18, 2008. http://query.nytimes.com/gst /fullpage.html?res=9D04E3DD103DF935A2575BC0A96E9 C8B63&scp=3&sq=Huntington%27s+Disease&st=nyt.

University of Leicester *Newsblog*, "Leicester's Fruit Flies Offer New Hope for Huntington's Disease," June 2, 2011. www2.le.ac.uk /news/blog/2011-archive/june/drosophila.

INDEX